Afternoon
tea at home

WILL TORRENT

Afternoon
tea at home

Deliciously indulgent
recipes for sandwiches,
savouries, scones, cakes
and other fancies

photography by Matt Russell

RYLAND PETERS & SMALL
LONDON • NEW YORK

For my wonderful wife.
Colossians 3: 12–17 x

Senior Designer Megan Smith
Commissioning Editor
Stephanie Milner
Picture Manager Christina Borsi
Head of Production
Patricia Harrington
Art Director Leslie Harrington
Editorial Director Julia Charles
Publisher Cindy Richards

Recipe Writer and Developer
Annie Rigg
Food Stylist Will Torrent
Prop Stylist Joanna Harris
Assistant Food Stylists
Jack Sargeson and Kathy Kordalis
Indexer Hilary Bird

First published in 2016 by
Ryland Peters & Small
20–21 Jockey's Fields,
London WC1R 4BW
and
341 E 116th St
New York NY 10029
www.rylandpeters.com

Text © Will Torrent 2016

Design and commissioned
photographs © Ryland Peters
& Small 2016

Picture credits
Page 8 above left ©
Bettmann/CORBIS;
Page 8 above right Topfoto;
Page 8 below Roger-
Viollet/Topfoto

ISBN: 978-1-84975-702-7

Printed and bound in China

10 9 8 7 6 5 4 3

A CIP record for this book
is available from the British
Library. US Library of Congress
Cataloging-in-Publication Data
has been applied for.

NOTES
• Both British (Metric) and
American (Imperial plus US cups)
measurements and ingredients
are included in these recipes for
your convenience, however it is
important to work with one set of
measurements and not alternate
between the two within a recipe.
• All spoon measurements are
level unless otherwise specified.
• All eggs are medium (UK) or
large (US), unless specified as
large, in which case US extra-large
should be used. Uncooked or
partially cooked eggs should not
be served to the very old, frail,
young children, pregnant women
or those with compromised
immune systems.
• When a recipe calls for the
zest of citrus fruit, buy unwaxed
fruit and wash well before using.
If you can only find treated fruit,
scrub well in warm soapy water
before using.
• Ovens should be preheated
to the specified temperatures.
We recommend using an oven
thermometer. If using a fan-
assisted oven, adjust temperatures
according to the manufacturer's
instructions.

Contents

Introduction

Afternoon tea is one of my favourite ways to eat. It's quintessentially British, has natural pomp and circumstance, oozes elegance and is defined by indulgence. It's been around since the 1800s but it is in the last few years that afternoon tea has had a resurgence. In grand venues such as 5-star hotels, riverside restaurants or boutique department stores, it can be a way to celebrate birthdays and engagements, get together with friends or even serve as a wedding breakfast – people just seem to love afternoon tea.

It is the delicate touches of small finger sandwiches (rectangular or triangular but always with the crusts cut off), little savouries, light and fluffy scones with clotted cream and jam/jelly, fine and elegant pâtisserie, a wide variety of teas and the occasional glass of fizz that people adore. But it's not just the food: the ornate and stunning locations that host afternoon tea are a luxury that can be recreated at home with an eye on the details – you might even feel like you're in Downton Abbey. I love the feeling of tranquillity and peace that contradicts the buzz of being served afternoon tea – nothing quite beats it.

There are two questions that need to be answered though; how do you pronounce 'scone' and should you layer cream on first or jam/jelly? Well, when it comes to the toppings, I'll explain that later on (there are lots of ways to serve a scone), but when it comes to how to pronounce the word 'scone', I do love this little poem that gives you a hint;

I asked the maid in dulcet tone
To order me a buttered scone;
The silly girl has been and gone
And ordered me a buttered scone. (Anon.)

Will Torrent

Time for tea

Afternoon tea has been around since the 1800s and was traditionally served between the hours of 4 pm and 7 pm, however these days, most establishments prefer to serve afternoon tea from lunchtime onwards, and continue until it's time to begin their evening dinner service.

With the rise in popularity of tea drinking in the 19th century, it is said that Anna, the 7th Duchess of Bedford and other ladies of the upper social classes would get a little peckish ahead of dinner. The solution was to have a cup of tea and a light snack mid-afternoon to keep the hunger pangs at bay. This soon became part of a daily routine and the Duchess began to invite friends to the house to join her for refreshment, and the rest, as they say, is history. However, it was thanks to Queen Victoria that afternoon tea came to be the more formal affair we enjoy today. During her reign, tea service became increasingly grand and enjoying the ritual in the country's celebrated dining rooms held social status. Etiquette played a big part, from the dress code to the way that tea was poured and stirred.

Today there are no strict rules when serving an afternoon tea, but traditionally it will consist of an ornate 3-tiered cake stand displaying a selection of dainty finger sandwiches and other small savouries, warm scones with accompanying pots of clotted cream and preserves, and a variety of visually appealing bite-size cakes and pastries. This enticing spread will be accompanied by your choice of a pot of freshly brewed loose-leaf tea, usually Earl Grey, Darjeeling and Assam are offered. Throughout this book you'll find both traditional recipes and my own ideas for teatime fancies, designed to be enjoyed throughout the seasons. Why not use the Menu Planners on pages 168–171 to put together your own bespoke selection of treats for any occasion?

Henry James (1843–1916), the great American writer who spent most of his writing life in England said: *'There are few hours in life more agreeable than the hour dedicated to the ceremony known as afternoon tea.'*
I certainly agree.

Clockwise from top left: An interior view of the famed The Ritz London hotel corridor where people are having afternoon tea; the Brown Derby Tea Room in Edinburgh, Scotland, overlooking Princes Street and Castle Rock (c. 1950); ladies drinking some tea in the garden of The Ritz Paris, 1st arrondissement (1930).

Afternoon tea essentials

A traditional afternoon tea requires basic condiments to be
served alongside the delicate plates of food. These can of course
be bought – there are many good-quality jams/jellies, curds,
spreads and butters available in stores – but if you really want
to go all out, try one of the recipes from these pages. Jam sugar
has added pectin which helps to set the mixture.

Jams and jellies

STRAWBERRY AND CHAMPAGNE
750 g/7½ cups
    strawberries
500 g/2½ cups jam sugar
200 ml/¾ cup
    Champagne
juice of 1 lemon

BLACKCURRANT AND CASSIS
750 g/7½ cups
    blackcurrants
500 g/2½ cups jam sugar
100 ml/⅓ cup water
100 ml/⅓ cup cassis

CHERRY AND KIRSCH
750 g/7½ cups fresh
    pitted/stoned cherries
500 g/2½ cups jam sugar
100 ml/⅓ cup water
100 ml/⅓ cup Kirsch

APRICOT AND VANILLA
750 g/7½ cups fresh
    pitted/stoned apricots
500 g/2½ cups jam sugar
200 ml/¾ cup orange
    juice
juice of 1 lemon
1 vanilla pod/bean, seeds
    scraped out

a sugar thermometer
a chilled plate or saucer

Each makes about
750 g/1¾ lbs.

For each of the jams/jellies, put all the ingredients into a large pan set over a medium heat and cook to 112°C (234°F) on a sugar thermometer. This is the 'setting' stage.

To test for a set, drop ½ teaspoon of the mixture onto a chilled plate, leave it for 30 seconds, then gently push it with your fingertip. If it wrinkles then it is ready, if not, continue to cook the jam/jelly for another 2 minutes and test again.

Remove the pan from the heat and set aside for 2–3 minutes before pouring into sterilized glass jars. Secure the lid on tightly, turn the jar upside down and leave to cool completely. This will create an airtight seal so you can store the jams/jellies outside of the fridge. Remember to label each jar so you know what you have and when you made it. Store in the cupboard for up to 6 months. Refrigerate once open and consume within 4 weeks.

The Dorchester Lemon curd

4 g/2 sheets leaf gelatin
300 ml/1¼ cup lemon juice
5 eggs, beaten
160 ml/⅔ cup clear honey
150 g/1 stick plus
    2 tablespoons butter

a sugar thermometer

Makes about 350 g/¾ lb.

To make the lemon curd, soak the gelatin in cold water for 10 minutes.

Put the lemon juice in a pan over a medium heat and warm through. In a large mixing bowl, whisk the beaten eggs and honey together, then pour into the pan with the lemon juice. Bring to the boil, stirring all the time. Cook for 1 minute then remove from the heat.

Drain the gelatin and squeeze off any excess water before adding to the pan. Bring to the boil, then cool down to about 40°C (104°F) when tested using a sugar thermometer. Add the butter and stir until completely melted. For best results blend to create an emulsion.

Passionfruit curd

100 g/½ cup caster/granulated sugar
75 g/5 tablespoons butter
a pinch of salt
pulp and seeds of 8 passionfruits
2 eggs, lightly beaten
2 egg yolks

Makes about 350 g/¾ lb.

Put the sugar, butter and salt into a heatproof bowl suspended over a pan of simmering water. Do not allow the underside of the bowl to come into contact with the water. When the butter has melted and the sugar is dissolved, add the passionfruit, beaten eggs and yolks. Continue to cook over a low heat stirring almost constantly until the curd is silky smooth, hot to the touch and has thickened enough to coat the back of a spoon.

Remove from the heat and pass though a fine mesh sieve/strainer into a clean bowl. Cover the surface of the curd with clingfilm/plastic wrap to prevent a skin forming and leave to cool for 10 minutes.

Use immediately or pour the curd into sterilized glass jars. Secure the lid on tightly, turn the jar upside down and leave to cool completely. This will create an airtight seal so you can store the jams/jellies outside of the fridge. Remember to label each jar so you know what you have and when you made it. Store in the cupboard for up to 2 months. Refrigerate once open and consume within 3 weeks.

Lime and yuzu curd

2 tablespoons yuzu juice (available online
   or in good Japanese supermarkets)
zest and juice of 2 limes
3 egg yolks
100 g/½ cup golden caster/raw cane sugar
2 tablespoons butter, chilled and diced

Makes about 350 g/¾ lb.

Put the yuzu juice with the lime zest and juice in a pan set over a low heat and slowly bring to the boil.

Put the egg yolks and sugar in a large mixing bowl and whisk with a balloon whisk until it looks like the sugar has dissolved. Very slowly pour the boiled citrus juice into the mixing bowl, whisking constantly.

Pour the mixture back into the pan, set over medium heat and stir. It will start to thicken and resemble thick, glossy curd. Remove it from the heat and whisk in the butter, one piece at a time. Mix until all the butter has melted.

Use immediately or pour the curd into sterilized glass jars. Secure the lid on tightly, turn the jar upside down and leave to cool completely. This will create an airtight seal so you can store the jams/jellies outside of the fridge. Remember to label each jar so you know what you have and when you made it. Store in the cupboard for up to 2 months. Refrigerate once open and consume within 3 weeks.

Rhubarb jam

1 kg/2 lbs. 3 oz. pink rhubarb,
   trimmed into 2-cm/¾-inch pieces
   (trimmed weight)
1 kg/5 cups jam sugar
zest and juice of 1 lemon

a sugar thermometer
a chilled plate or saucer

Makes about 1 kg/2¼ lbs.

Tip the trimmed rhubarb into a large mixing bowl and add the sugar, lemon zest and juice and stir well to combine.

Cover the bowl with clingfilm/plastic wrap and leave for at least 2 hours but preferably overnight to allow the sugar to dissolve into the rhubarb juices. Stir the mixture a couple of times to speed the process along.

Scoop the fruit and all of the sugary juices into a pan and set over a medium heat. Stir to dissolve any remaining sugar and bring to the boil. Continue to cook at a fairly swift pace for 10–15 minutes until the rhubarb is really tender and the mixture has reached setting point – 112°C (234°F) – on a sugar thermometer.

To test for a set, drop ½ teaspoon of the mixture onto a chilled plate, leave it for 30 seconds, then gently push it with your fingertip. If it wrinkles then it is ready, if not, continue to cook the jam/jelly for another 2 minutes and test again.

Remove the pan from the heat and set aside for 2–3 minutes before pouring into sterilized glass jars. Secure the lid on tightly, turn the jar upside down and leave to cool completely. This will create an airtight seal so you can store the jam/jelly outside of the fridge. Remember to label each jar so you know what you have and when you made it. Store in the cupboard for up to 6 months. Refrigerate once open and consume within 4 weeks.

Cherry compote

175 ml/scant ¾ cup red wine
juice of 1 orange plus 2 strips of peel
1 bay leaf
1 cinnamon stick
½ vanilla pod/bean, split
1 star anise
30 g/2½ tablespoons caster/
   granulated sugar
2 teaspoons cornflour/cornstarch
2 teaspoons Kirsch or cherry brandy
a 400-g/14-oz. can dark cherries in syrup,
   drained and patted dry

Makes 500 g/1¼ lbs.

Tip the red wine into a small pan, add the orange juice and orange peel, the bay leaf, cinnamon stick, vanilla pod/bean, star anise and sugar. Set over a medium heat stirring to dissolve the sugar. Bring to the boil and simmer gently until reduced to 3 tablespoons of thick syrup. Pass the mixture through a fine mesh sieve/strainer into a clean bowl to remove the spices and peel, then return the syrup to the pan.

In a small bowl, combine the cornflour/cornstarch with the Kirsch or cherry brandy and mix to a smooth paste. Spoon the paste into the red wine syrup and whisk to combine. Cook over a low–medium heat until thickened and glossy and you can no longer taste the cornflour/cornstarch. Add the cherries and cook for a further minute to break down the fruit slightly.

Remove the pan from the heat and cool completely before using. Store the compote in an airtight container in the fridge for up to 1 week.

Chocolate and espresso 'curd'

125 g/1 stick plus ¾ tablespoon butter, chilled and diced
50 ml/scant ¼ cup espresso
70 g/½ cup chopped dark/bittersweet chocolate (80%)
4 egg yolks
100 g/½ cup white sugar

Makes about 350 g/¾ lb.

Put the butter into a large mixing bowl, followed by the espresso and chopped chocolate. Suspend the bowl over a pan of simmering water and whisk the ingredients together. Add the egg yolks and sugar and stir continuously over the heat to combine. When the curd starts to leave a trail from the whisk this means it's starting to cook through – you'll find the edges cook first so run your whisk around the inside of the bowl to make sure it does not get too hot too quickly.

Pour a spoonful of the curd onto a plate and pop it into the fridge for a few minutes. When cool, run your finger through the middle of the curd and if it stays separate then it is cooked.

Use immediately or pour the curd into sterilized glass jars. Secure the lid on tightly, turn the jar upside down and leave to cool completely. This will create an airtight seal so you can store the curd outside of the fridge. Remember to label each jar so you know what you have and when you made it. Store in the cupboard for up to 1 week. Refrigerate once open and consume within 3 days.

Chocolate and hazelnut spread

50 g/½ cup hazelnut paste
50 g/⅓ cup finely chopped milk/semi-sweet chocolate
50 g/⅓ cup finely chopped dark/bittersweet chocolate
100 ml/6 tablespoons double/heavy cream
30 ml/2 tablespoons hazelnut oil

Makes about 250 g/9 oz.

Put the cream and oil in a pan and set over a medium heat to warm through. Add all the chocolate. Stir to melt the chocolate and combine.

Blitz with a handheld electric blender before transferring to a sterilized glass jar.

Use immediately or pour the spread into sterilized glass jars. Secure the lid on tightly, turn the jar upside down and leave to cool completely. This will create an airtight seal so you can store the spread outside of the fridge. Remember to label each jar so you know what you have and when you made it. Store in the cupboard for up to 1 week. Refrigerate once open and consume within 3 days.

VARIATION
Chocolate and pistachios also work incredibly well together and you can simply replace the hazelnut paste with pistachio purée/paste and use groundnut oil instead of the hazelnut oil.

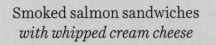

Smoked salmon sandwiches
with whipped cream cheese

Roast beef sandwiches

Devilled egg mayonnaise
sandwiches *with micro herbs*

Cucumber sandwiches
with yuzu and chive butter

Classic scones

The Ritz London Fruited scones

Viennese whirls

Simple vanilla shortbreads

Cherry and almond Bakewell tarts

Chocolate and peanut butter délices

Victoria sponge *with strawberry
jam and vanilla buttercream*

Classic
afternoon
tea

Smoked salmon and cream cheese is one of those match-made-in-heaven combinations and by whipping the cream cheese a bit, the sandwich becomes delightfully light. The ultimate roast beef sandwich has to be made with thinly sliced, roast beef. With a horseradish and onion confit mayonnaise and crisp watercress it's a proper British sandwich.

Smoked salmon sandwiches
with whipped cream cheese

150 g/1 stick plus
   2 tablespoons butter,
   softened
1 teaspoon lemon zest
   and 2 teaspoons juice
salt and freshly ground
   black pepper, to taste
300 g/10 oz. cream
   cheese
8 thin slices brown bread
400 g/14 oz. thinly sliced
   smoked salmon

Makes 24

Beat the butter until really soft and spreadable, add the lemon zest and juice, season with salt and black pepper and mix in.

In another bowl beat the cream cheese with a wooden spoon or rubber spatula until really light, season with black pepper and mix well.

Lay the bread out on the work surface and spread with a thin layer of the lemon butter. Spread half of the slices with the whipped cream cheese and lay the smoked salmon on the remaining buttered slices of bread.

Sandwich the two together and using a serrated knife trim off the crusts.

Cut each sandwich into dainty bite-sized rectangles or triangles to serve.

Roast beef sandwiches

1 onion
2 garlic cloves
1 tablespoon olive oil
salt and freshly ground
   black pepper, to taste
1–2 teaspoons creamed
   horseradish
4 tablespoons
   mayonnaise
10 slices white bread
75 g/5 tablespoons salted
   butter, softened
15 thin slices roast beef
fresh watercress

Makes 24

Preheat the oven to 190°C (375°F) Gas 5.

Lay a sheet of foil in a roasting pan and put the whole onion and garlic cloves on top, drizzle with the olive oil, season with salt and black pepper and wrap up tightly. Cook on the middle shelf of the preheated oven for about 40 minutes until caramelized.

Leave to cool slightly, then scoop the onion and garlic flesh from the skins into a food processor. Pulse until roughly chopped and leave to cool to room temperature.

Combine the mayonnaise and horseradish in a small bowl, add the onion and garlic mixture and stir until combined. Lay the bread out on the work surface and spread half of them with butter. Spread the remaining bread slices with the onion mayonnaise. You may have more mayonnaise than needed but you can keep it in the fridge for 1–2 days.

Lay the beef over the mayonnaise, top with watercress, then with the buttered bread, butter-side down and press the slices gently together. Trim off the crusts and cut the sandwiches into triangles or rectangles.

Give the humble egg mayo sandwich a new lease of life by adding spices, Dijon mustard and a little mango chutney in a nod to the retro devilled egg. Or dress thinly sliced cucumber in cider vinegar – it lightly pickles it and gives the sandwich a little lift, which works really well with the citrus butter.

Devilled egg mayonnaise sandwiches *with micro herbs*

4 eggs
a pinch of salt
2–3 tablespoons mayonnaise
1 tablespoon mango chutney
1 teaspoon Dijon mustard
½ teaspoon cayenne pepper or paprika
freshly ground black pepper, to taste
50 g/3½ tablespoons salted butter, softened
8 slices white bread
fresh watercress

Makes 16

Carefully arrange the eggs in a saucepan in which they will fit snuggly. Add the salt and cover with cold water. Bring to the boil, then reduce the heat and simmer for 6 minutes. Drain and run cold water over the eggs for at least 3 minutes until they are completely cold.

Peel the eggs, finely chop and tip into a bowl. Add the mayonnaise, mango chutney, mustard, cayenne pepper or paprika and season with salt and black pepper. Mix well.

Lay the bread out on the work surface and spread with butter. Divide the egg mixture between half of the slices, spreading it evenly and scatter with watercress. Top with the other buttered slices, butter-side down and gently press together.

Using a serrated knife trim off the crusts. Cut each sandwich into dainty bite-sized triangles or rectangles to serve.

Cucumber sandwiches *with yuzu and chive butter*

100 g/7 tablespoons butter, softened
2 teaspoons yuzu or lemon juice
1 tablespoon finely chopped fresh chives
salt and freshly ground black pepper, to taste
½ large cucumber
2 teaspoons cider vinegar
8 slices white bread

Makes 24

Beat the butter until really soft and spreadable. Gradually add the yuzu or lemon juice, mix in and season with salt and black pepper. Add the chives and mix to combine.

Peel the cucumber and thinly slice into rounds. Tip the slices into a bowl, add the cider vinegar and toss to coat.

Lay half of the bread slices out on the work surface and spread with half of the yuzu and chive butter.

Arrange the cucumber slices on top as neatly and evenly as possible and season with salt and pepper. Spread the remaining bread with the yuzu and chive butter and press on top of the cucumber-topped bread, butter-side down.

Gently press the sandwiches together and trim off the crusts using a serrated knife.

Cut the sandwiches into neat rectangles or triangles to serve.

You can't have afternoon tea without scones, and they have to be served with clotted cream and jam/jelly, and, for me, it has to be homemade and strawberry-flavoured! Now, depending on where you come from in the South West of England, that will decide whether to have spread the jam/jelly or cream on first? In Devon, it's cream first and in Cornwall it's the other way round. As long as it comes with both, either way round is good for me!

Classic scones

450 g/3½ cups plain/
all-purpose flour
3 teaspoons baking
powder
a pinch of salt
100 g/7 tablespoons
butter, chilled and
diced
75 g/generous ⅓ cup
caster/granulated
sugar
2 egg yolks
250 ml/1 cup whole milk,
plus extra for glazing
1 teaspoon lemon juice

TO SERVE
good-quality strawberry
jam/jelly (page 11)
clotted cream or
whipped double/heavy
cream

*a 5-cm/2-inch round
cookie cutter
a baking sheet lined
with baking parchment*

Makes about 24

Preheat the oven to 220°C (425°F) Gas 7.

Sift the flour into a large mixing bowl with the baking powder and salt. Add the butter. Start by using a palette knife to cut the butter into the flour, then switch to using your hands to gently rub the butter in. Do not overwork the mixture but lift the flour and butter up in your hands and gently press and roll it across your fingertips. When there are no visible pieces of butter remaining add the sugar and mix to combine.

Make a well in the middle of the mixture and add 1 of the egg yolks, the milk and lemon juice. Use the palette knife to cut the wet ingredients into the dry, then gently mix with your hands until almost combined.

Turn the dough out onto a lightly floured work surface. Very gently knead until almost smooth. Pat or roll the dough to a thickness of 3 cm/1¼ inches.

Dip the cookie cutter in flour to prevent it sticking, then stamp out discs from the dough. Arrange them on the prepared baking sheet and set aside. Gather the off-cuts of dough into a ball, re-roll and stamp out more scones to make as many as possible.

Mix the remaining egg yolk with 1 tablespoon of milk and neatly brush the tops of the scones with the glaze.

Bake on the middle shelf of the preheated oven for about 10 minutes until well-risen and golden brown.

Remove from the oven, cool on wire racks and serve on the day of making with jam/jelly and clotted cream.

The Ritz has been serving Afternoon Tea since it opened its doors in 1906 and remains *the* place for the quintessentially British afternoon tea. An institution in itself; songs, books and more have been written about The Ritz. Last year alone over 14,000 guests took tea in the glamorous setting of The Palm Court; the world-class service and ornate settings will make you feel like royalty. Gentleman, you will need a tie and ladies, dress in your best! John Williams MBE, Executive Chef, and his team make an incredible 1,200 scones every day and these popular scones have never left the menu.

Fruited scones

400 g/3 cups strong/ bread flour
60 g/scant ⅓ cup caster/granulated sugar
30 g/3 tablespoons baking powder
a small pinch of salt
60 g/½ stick butter
250 ml/1 cup buttermilk
100 g/¾ cup (dark) raisins
1 beaten egg, for glazing

TO SERVE
good-quality jam/jelly of your choosing (pages 11–14)
clotted cream

a 5-cm/2-inch round cookie cutter
a baking sheet lined with baking parchment

Makes about 24

Put the flour, sugar, baking powder, salt and butter in a large mixing bowl. Mix together with your fingertips to the consistency of fine breadcrumbs. Add the buttermilk and gently stir to combine until a dough forms. Add the raisins and knead lightly to spread them throughout the dough. Don't overwork the dough – the less you work it the more light and fluffy the scones will be. Cover the bowl and set aside to rest for 10 minutes. This allows the dough to relax to avoid toughness.

Turn the dough out onto a lightly floured work surface and roll out to a thickness of 1 cm/⅜ inch. Stamp out rounds using the cookie cutter, turn them over and arrange on the prepared baking sheet. Bring any scraps of dough together, re-roll and stamp out as many rounds as you can.

Brush the tops of each round with a little beaten egg to glaze.

Cover the sheets with a clean kitchen cloth and set aside in a warm place to rise and prove for 30 minutes.

Preheat the oven to 160°C (325°F) Gas 3.

Bake the scones in the preheated oven for about 30 minutes until a skewer inserted into the middle of a scone comes out clean. Transfer to a wire rack to cool.

Serve warm or cold with jam/jelly and clotted cream on the side.

Beating the butter and sugar for as long as you can, helps give these beautiful little biscuits their melt-in-your-mouth texture and sandwiched with oozing raspberry jam/jelly and vanilla buttercream, they certainly won't last long on your cake stand!

Viennese whirls

200 g/1 stick plus 5½ tablespoons butter, softened

75 g/½ cup icing/confectioners' sugar

1 teaspoon vanilla bean paste

200 g/1²⁄₃ cups plain/all-purpose flour

30 g/3 tablespoons cornflour/cornstarch

½ teaspoon baking powder

a pinch of salt

1–2 tablespoons whole milk

BUTTERCREAM

75 g/5 tablespoons butter, softened

150 g/1 cup icing/confectioners' sugar, plus extra for dusting

½ teaspoon vanilla bean paste

3–4 tablespoons good-quality raspberry jam/jelly

2 large piping/pastry bags fitted with a large star nozzle/tips

2 baking sheets lined with baking parchment

Makes 12–16

The butter for these biscuits must be very soft so if necessary give it a 10-second burst in the microwave to soften it. Tip the butter into the bowl of a stand mixer, add the icing/confectioners' sugar and beat for at least 3 minutes until really pale, soft and light. Add the vanilla bean paste and mix in.

Sift the flour, cornflour/cornstarch, baking powder and salt into the bowl. Add 1 tablespoon of the milk and mix until smooth and thoroughly combined. If the mixture looks a little stiff add a little more milk to loosen it. Spoon the mixture into one of the piping/pastry bags and pipe even rounds onto the prepared baking sheets leaving a little space between each one to allow for spreading during cooking.

Chill the whirls in the fridge for 30 minutes.

Preheat the oven to 170°C (325°F) Gas 3.

Bake on the middle shelf in the preheated oven for 10–12 minutes until firm and starting to turn golden brown at the edges. Leave to cool on the baking sheets for 3 minutes, then transfer to a wire rack to cool completely.

Meanwhile, prepare the buttercream. Put the butter and icing/confectioners' sugar in a large mixing bowl and cream together until really pale and light. Add the vanilla bean paste and mix again to combine. Spoon the buttercream into the remaining piping/pastry bag.

Turn all of the biscuits upside down so that they are flat-side uppermost and pipe half of them with a swirl of buttercream. Spread the remaining biscuits with raspberry jam/jelly and sandwich them together.

Dust with icing/confectioners' sugar to serve.

These are always my go-to quick biscuit bake – there's nothing better than shortbread and tea! Simple. Shortbread is so good at taking on other flavours, from lemon and orange zest to warming Christmas spices, it's just so versatile.

Simple vanilla shortbreads

300 g/2 sticks plus 5 tablespoons butter, softened
150 g/¾ cup caster/superfine sugar, plus extra for sprinkling
zest of 1 lemon
seeds from ½ vanilla pod/bean or 1 teaspoon vanilla bean paste
400 g/3 cups plain/all-purpose flour, plus extra for rolling out
a pinch of salt

a 5-cm/2-inch round cookie cutter
2 baking sheets lined with baking parchment

Makes about 40

Tip the butter into the bowl of a stand mixer. Add the sugar and beat for 3–4 minutes until pale and light. Add the lemon zest and seeds from the vanilla pod/bean or vanilla bean paste and mix in.

Sift in the flour and salt and mix again until smooth and thoroughly combined.

Tip the dough out and shape into a neat rectangle roughly 2 cm/¾ inch thick. Wrap in clingfilm/plastic wrap and chill in the fridge for at least 4 hours.

Remove the dough from the fridge 20 minutes before you plan on rolling it out to allow it to soften slightly.

Lightly dust the work surface with flour and cut the dough in half – this will make rolling out easier. Roll out the dough into a neat rectangle roughly 8 cm/3¼ inch wide and 1 cm/⅜ inch thick.

Stamp out rounds using the cookie cutter and arrange on the prepared baking sheets, leaving a little space between each for spreading. Bring together the scraps of dough, re-roll and stamp out as many rounds as possible. Prick the rounds with a fork and chill in the fridge for 30 minutes.

Preheat the oven to 160°C (325°F) Gas 3.

Bake the shortbreads on the middle shelf of the preheated oven for about 15 minutes until crisp and starting to turn golden brown at the edges.

Remove from the oven, sprinkle with caster/superfine sugar and leave to cool on the baking sheets for 10 minutes.

Transfer to a wire rack to cool completely and serve.

Cherry and almond Bakewell tarts

3 tablespoons good-
   quality cherry jam/jelly
   (page 11)
50 g/⅔ cup flaked/
   slivered almonds
3–4 glacé cherries

ALMOND PASTRY
175 g/1⅓ cups plain/
   all-purpose flour
25 g/¼ cup ground
   almonds
a pinch of salt
100 g/7 tablespoons
   butter, chilled and diced
25 g/2½ tablespoons
   icing/confectioners'
   sugar
1 egg, lightly beaten

FRANGIPANE
50 g/3½ tablespoons
   butter, softened
50 g/¼ cup caster/
   granulated sugar
1 egg and 1 egg yolk,
   lightly beaten
1 teaspoon vanilla extract
50 g/½ cup ground
   almonds
20 g/1½ tablespoons
   plain/all-purpose flour

FROSTING
100 g/⅔ cup icing/
   confectioners' sugar
½ teaspoon almond
   extract

*a 10-cm/4-inch round
cookie cutter
12–15 x 7-cm/3-inch fluted
tart pans or a 12-hole
muffin pan, greased*

Makes 12

One of my favourite tea-time treats, these little Bakewell tarts celebrate the wonderful combination of cherries and almond. A crisp almond pastry, cherry and amaretto jam/jelly, soft buttery frangipane, topped with almond-flavoured icing, with crystallized almonds and a little slither of a glacé cherry!

Start by making the almond pastry. Tip the flour and ground almonds into the bowl of the food processor, add the salt and the butter. Using the pulse button rub the butter into the flour until it is pale sand-like in texture. Add the icing/confectioners' sugar and pulse again to combine. Add the beaten egg and pulse again until the dough starts to come together.

Tip out onto the work surface and use your hands to bring it together into a neat ball. Flatten into a disc, cover in clingfilm/plastic wrap and chill for at least 1 hour until firm.

Meanwhile prepare the frangipane. Cream the butter with the caster/granulated sugar until pale and light. Gradually add the beaten egg and egg yolk, mixing well between each addition. Add the vanilla extract and mix to combine. Tip the ground almonds and flour into the bowl and mix until smooth.

Roll out the chilled pastry on a lightly floured work surface to a thickness of no more than 2 mm/¹⁄₁₆ inch. Stamp out as many discs as you can using the cookie cutter. Gather the scraps together, re-roll and stamp out more discs. Gently press the pastry discs into the tart pans, trying not to stretch the dough but making sure that the pans are evenly lined.

Arrange the pans on a baking sheet and chill for 20 minutes while you preheat the oven to 170°C (350°F) Gas 3. Place another solid baking sheet on the middle shelf of the oven to heat up while it preheats.

Spread ½ teaspoon of jam/jelly into the bottom of each tart shell and divide the frangipane evenly between the tarts – spreading it to evenly cover the jam/jelly. Carefully transfer the individual pans to the hot baking sheet from the oven and bake in the preheated oven for about 20 minutes until the frangipane and pastry are golden and the pastry is crisp.

While the oven is hot, lightly toast the almonds on a baking sheet for 4 minutes until golden. Leave the tarts to cool in the pans for 30 minutes, then transfer to a wire rack to cool completely.

To make the frosting, sift the icing/confectioners' sugar into a bowl, add a drop or two of almond extract and enough water to make a smooth liquid that will coat the back of a spoon. Neatly spoon the icing over the frangipane in each tart and press the toasted almond bits around the edge. Top each tart with a slither of glacé cherry and leave to set before serving.

Chocolate and peanut butter délices

This naughty little slice takes its inspiration from Devil's food cake (a rich chocolatey cake with bittersweet chocolatey frosting) paired with my favourite flavour, peanut butter. It's rich and indulgent and not for the faint-hearted. If you don't want to use peanut butter you can use a drop of coffee and extra cream cheese for a twist on a classic Gâteau Opera.

150 g/1 cup plus
  2 tablespoons plain/
  all-purpose flour
40 g/⅓ cup cocoa powder
1 teaspoon baking powder
½ teaspoon bicarbonate
  of soda/baking soda
a pinch of salt
125 g/scant ⅔ cup caster/
  granulated sugar
100 g/½ cup soft light
  brown sugar
100 ml/⅓ cup whole milk
75 ml/5 tablespoons
  sunflower oil
1 large egg, lightly beaten
1 teaspoon vanilla extract
100 ml/⅓ cup hot coffee
gold leaf, to decorate

HONEY-ROASTED PEANUTS
100 g/¾ cup salted
  peanuts
1 tablespoon clear honey

FROSTING
250 g/8 oz. cream cheese
175 g/¾ cup smooth
  peanut butter
25 g/1½ tablespoons
  butter, softened
50 g/⅓ cup icing/
  confectioners' sugar
25 g/2 tablespoons soft
  light brown sugar
1 teaspoon vanilla extract
1 tablespoon whole milk

CHOCOLATE GLAZE
100 g/3½ oz. dark/
  bittersweet chocolate
45 g/3 tablespoons butter
40 g/¼ cup whole milk
1 tablespoon clear honey

*a 20 x 30-cm/8 x 12-inch
baking pan lined with
baking parchment*

Makes 12 slices

Preheat the oven to 180°C (350°F) Gas 4.

Sift the flour, cocoa powder, baking powder, bicarbonate of soda/baking soda and salt into the bowl of a stand mixer fitted with a whisk attachment. Add the caster/granulated and soft light brown sugars and make a well in the middle. Add the milk, sunflower oil, beaten egg and vanilla extract before adding the hot coffee. Beat well for about 2 minutes until smooth. Pour into the prepared baking pan.

Bake on the middle shelf of the preheated oven for about 20 minutes until well risen and a skewer inserted into the middle of the cake comes out clean.

Rest in the pan for 3 minutes, then transfer to a wire rack to cool completely.

While the oven is still hot, prepare the honey-roasted peanuts. Tip the peanuts onto a non-stick baking sheet, drizzle over the honey and mix to coat. Toast in the oven for about 4 minutes until golden brown and caramelized. You will need to give the nuts a stir halfway through cooking to ensure that they caramelize evenly. Cool completely, roughly chop and set aside until needed.

To make the frosting, scoop the cream cheese, peanut butter and butter into a large mixing bowl and beat until smooth. Sift over the icing/confectioners' sugar, soft light brown sugar, vanilla extract and milk and beat again until smooth and creamy.

Using a serrated bread knife, carefully slice the cake lengthways into three layers. It is easiest to do this when the cake is chilled so once completely cold you could refrigerate or freeze it for 30 minutes to firm up.

Spread the frosting on top of each layer using a palette knife. Carefully place one layer on top of another and sandwich together.

To make the chocolate glaze, combine all the ingredients in a small pan set over a low–medium heat and cook until smooth and shiny. Cool slightly, then pour the glaze over the top of the layered cakes and spread one each side.

Cut slices of about 3 x 6 cm/1¼ x 2½ inches. Decorate with honey-roasted peanuts and a little gold leaf.

Victoria sponge *with strawberry jam and vanilla buttercream*

225 g/1 stick plus
  7 tablespoons butter,
  softened
225 g/1 cup plus
  2 tablespoons caster/
  granulated sugar
1 teaspoon vanilla bean
  paste
4 large eggs, lightly
  beaten
175 g/1⅓ cups plain/
  all-purpose flour
50 g/⅓ cup cornflour/
  cornstarch
2 teaspoons baking
  powder
a pinch of salt
2–3 tablespoons whole
  milk
3–4 tablespoons good-
  quality strawberry
  jam/jelly (page 11),
  to serve

VANILLA BUTTERCREAM
150 g/1 stick plus
  2 tablespoons butter,
  softened
200 g/1⅓ cups icing/
  confectioners' sugar,
  plus extra for dusting
2 teaspoons vanilla bean
  paste

*2 x 20-cm/8-inch round
cake pans base-lined with
baking parchment*

Serves 8

Words cannot express my love for this most British of cakes! Named after Queen Victoria, it is simply one of the UK's most loved cakes baked for many years by families up and down the country. Sandwiched with homemade jam/jelly and lashings of vanilla buttercream, it's just wonderfully simple and very tempting, too!

Preheat the oven to 180°C (375°F) Gas 4.

Cream together the butter and caster/granulated sugar in a large mixing bowl until really pale and fluffy – this will take about 5 minutes. Add the vanilla bean paste, then gradually add the beaten eggs, a little at a time, mixing well between each addition and adding a little of the flour if the mixture looks curdled at any stage. Sift the flour, cornflour/cornstarch and baking powder into the bowl, add the salt, 2 tablespoons of the milk and mix again until smooth. Add extra milk if necessary to slacken the mixture.

Divide the batter evenly between the prepared cake pans and bake on the middle shelf of the preheated oven for about 30 minutes until pale golden and a skewer inserted in the middle of the cakes comes out clean.

Cool in the pans for 5 minutes, then turn out onto a wire rack until completely cold.

To make the vanilla buttercream, cream the butter in a stand mixer until very soft and pale. Sift in the icing/confectioners' sugar and vanilla bean paste in stages, mixing well between each addition until pale, smooth and very light. Spread the top of one of the cakes with the buttercream. Cover with a thick layer of strawberry jam/jelly and top with the other cake pressing down gently.

Dust with icing/confectioners' sugar and serve immediately.

Bloody Mary shrimp sandwich

Blueberry and buttermilk scones
with honeycomb butter

Raspberry and rose party hearts

The Dorchester 'Beehive' tarts

Jam tarts

Passionfruit meringue tarts

Lemon and polenta drizzle cakes

Carrot cake

Mocha mini cakes

Fruit cake *with an orange glaze*

Spring selection

The addition of some of the ingredients that make up a Bloody Mary cocktail to a classic Marie Rose sauce takes a simple prawn/shrimp sandwich to a whole new level. The crushed avocado butter elevates it even further, which in my opinion, when done right, is simply stunning.

Bloody Mary shrimp sandwich

400 g/14 oz. cooked north Atlantic prawns/shrimp
3 tablespoons mayonnaise
1 tablespoon ketchup
½ teaspoon paprika
a splash of Tabasco
1 tablespoon vodka (optional)
a dash of Worcestershire sauce
salt and freshly ground black pepper, to taste

AVOCADO BUTTER
75 g/5 tablespoons butter, softened
1 ripe avocado
juice of ½ lemon
salt and freshly ground black pepper, to taste

TO SERVE
8 thin slices brown bread
2 heads little Gem lettuce, shredded
celery salt, to taste

Makes 8

Pat the prawns/shrimp dry with paper towels and tip into a bowl. Add the mayonnaise, ketchup, paprika, Tabasco, vodka (if using) and a shake of Worcestershire sauce. Season with salt and black pepper, and mix well to coat the prawns/shrimp. Taste and add a drop more Tabasco if you prefer the Bloody Mary sauce a little spicier.

In another bowl, beat the butter until soft. Peel and mash the avocado flesh, and add to the butter with the lemon juice. Season with salt and black pepper to taste.

Lay the bread slices out on the work surface and spread with the avocado butter. Cover half of the slices with the prawn/shrimp mixture and top with a neat handful of shredded lettuce. Cover with the remaining bread slices and press gently together.

Using a serrated bread knife, cut the sandwiches in half or into neat triangles or fingers. Arrange on serving plates and sprinkle with a little celery salt before serving.

These are a weekend breakfast favourite of mine but are also perfect on an afternoon tea stand. Super simple to make and even quicker to eat... all of them! Serve warm from the oven with a dollop of honeycomb butter melting over the top – the perfect treat for a lazy weekend morning or leisurely tea. You can use frozen blueberries if you can't find fresh.

Blueberry and buttermilk scones
with honeycomb butter

350 g/2¾ cups plain/ all-purpose flour, plus extra for rolling out
3 teaspoons baking powder
a pinch of salt
125 g/1 stick butter, chilled and diced
75 g/generous ⅓ cup caster/granulated sugar
175–200 ml/⅔–¾ cup buttermilk
150 g/1¼ cup fresh or frozen blueberries
2 tablespoons whole milk
2 tablespoons demerara/ turbinado sugar

HONEYCOMB BUTTER
100 g/3½ oz. honeycomb or 2 chocolate-covered honeycomb bars
175 g/1½ sticks butter, softened
1 teaspoon vanilla bean paste
a pinch of salt

2 baking sheets lined with baking parchment

Makes 16

Start by making the honeycomb butter. Tip the honeycomb into a freezer bag, twist the end to prevent any escaping and crush the honeycomb using a rolling pin. Cream the butter and vanilla bean paste in a stand mixer until really soft. Add the crushed honeycomb and mix again until combined.

Lay a piece of clingfilm/plastic wrap or baking parchment on the work surface and spoon the butter down the middle to form a rough sausage shape, wrap up the butter tightly to make a smooth log, twist the ends to seal and put the butter in the fridge to harden until needed. Alternatively you can make the butter fresh while the scones are baking and use immediately.

Preheat the oven to 200°C (400°F) Gas 6.

Sift the flour, baking powder and a pinch of salt into a large mixing bowl. Add the chilled, diced butter and rub into the dry ingredients using your hands. When the mixture resembles sand and there are only very small pieces of butter remaining, add the caster/granulated sugar and mix to combine.

Make a well in the middle of the mixture, add the buttermilk and blueberries and stir to combine using a rubber spatula. Once the dough starts to come together, use your hands to form a rough ball.

Tip the dough out onto a lightly floured work surface. Very lightly knead for about 30 seconds to bring the dough into an almost smooth ball but do not overwork the dough. Cut in half and flatten each half into a round disc each about 16 cm/6¼ inches in diameter. Using a long, sharp knife cut each disc into 8 triangular wedge shapes.

Arrange the wedges on the prepared baking sheets and brush the tops with a little milk, scatter with demerara/turbinado sugar and bake on the middle shelf of the preheated oven for 12–14 minutes, or until well-risen and golden.

Cool on a wire rack and serve slightly warm with slices of the honeycomb butter ready to spread on top.

Raspberry and rose party hearts

25 g/2 tablespoons freeze-dried raspberries
100 g/⅔ cup icing/confectioners' sugar
200 g/1¾ sticks butter, softened
1 teaspoon vanilla extract
1 teaspoon rosewater
zest of ½ lemon
2 egg yolks, lightly beaten
250 g/2 cups plain/all-purpose flour
½ teaspoon baking powder
a pinch of salt

RASPBERRY ICING
125 g/1 cup fresh raspberries
1 teaspoon rosewater
400 g/3¼ cups royal icing sugar or 3 cups icing/confectioners' sugar plus 2½ tablespoons meringue powder
crystallized rose petals, to decorate

2 baking sheets lined with baking parchment
a heart-shaped cookie cutter
a disposable piping/pastry bag
toothpicks

Makes 25–30

When I was a kid, I used to love eating Party Ring biscuits at friends' birthdays, always trying to lick the icing off before either eating the biscuit or throwing it away. I'd like to think that my eating habits and tastes have improved since then, and these raspberry and rose party hearts are a delightful twist on a family favourite with a delicate rosewater and fresh raspberry icing, complete with feathered white decoration, of course!

Tip the freeze-dried raspberries into a food processor and pulse until very finely chopped. Set aside.

Put the icing/confectioners' sugar and butter in the bowl of a stand mixer and beat until pale and light. Add the vanilla extract, rosewater and lemon zest and mix in.

Add the beaten egg yolks a little at a time, mixing well between each addition. Sift in the flour, baking powder and salt. Add the chopped freeze-dried raspberries and mix gently to make a smooth dough – do not overwork the dough otherwise the biscuits will be tough rather than crisp and light. Gather the dough into a neat disc, wrap in clingfilm/plastic wrap and chill for at least 1 hour or until firm.

Roll the dough out on a lightly floured work surface to a thickness of 2–3 mm/⅛ inch. Stamp out biscuits using the cookie cutter and arrange on the prepared baking sheets. Chill for 15 minutes while you preheat the oven to 170°C (325°F) Gas 3.

Bake the biscuits on the middle shelf of the preheated oven for 12–14 minutes until crisp and starting to turn golden at the edges. Cool on the baking sheets for 5 minutes, then transfer to a wire rack to cool completely.

To prepare the raspberry icing, crush the raspberries with a fork, then push the fruit through a fine mesh sieve/strainer into a mixing bowl to remove all the seeds. Add the rosewater, then gradually add three-quarters of the royal icing sugar or icing/confectioners' sugar plus meringue powder to the raspberry mixture, whisking constantly until smooth and thick enough to coat the back of a spoon. You many need to add more or less royal icing sugar to achieve the correct consistency.

Tip the remaining royal icing sugar into a bowl and beating well, add enough water to make this the same thickness as the raspberry icing. Spoon the white icing into a disposable piping/pastry bag and snip the end into a fine point.

Taking one biscuit at a time dip the top into the raspberry icing to neatly coat, allow any excess icing to drip back into the bowl. Lay the iced biscuit back onto a clean sheet of baking parchment. Pipe neat thin lines of white icing across the pink heart. Take a toothpick and drag the point through the white icing to create a feathered effect. Repeat with the remaining hearts and attach a crystallized rose petal to each one while still wet. Leave to set firm before serving.

While at university, I had the amazing opportunity to work at The Dorchester as part of my training and I loved it! Used by the rich and the famous ever since it opened in 1931, the hotel's Head Pastry Chef David Girard, has presented afternoon tea to royalty including Her Majesty The Queen and uses over a ton of chocolate every year. This recipe is straight from their tea menu.

'Beehive' tarts

200 g/1²/₃ cups plain/ all-purpose flour
130 g/1 stick plus 1 tablespoon butter
90 g/¾ cup icing/ confectioners' sugar
60 g/²/₃ cup ground almonds
20 g/1½ tablespoons cocoa powder
a pinch of salt
4 egg yolks

HONEY CARAMEL
4 g/2 sheets leaf gelatin
160 g/½ cup honey
300 ml/1¼ cups double/heavy cream
a pinch of salt
90 g/6 tablespoons butter

TO DECORATE
lemon curd (page 11)
100 g/3½ oz. dark/ bittersweet chocolate
cocoa butter transfer sheet (page 172)
sugar bees (page 172)

a 5-cm/2-inch and 7-cm/ 3-inch cookie cutter
a 12-hole muffin pan, greased
baking beans (optional)
a disposable piping/pastry bag

Makes 12

Put the flour and butter in a large mixing bowl and work together with fingertips to the consistency of breadcrumbs. In a separate bowl, mix together the icing/confectioners' sugar, ground almonds, cocoa powder and salt. Slowly add this to the butter and flour mixture. Stir gently until combined, then add the egg yolks. Stir again to form a dough. Wrap in clingfilm/plastic wrap and chill in the fridge for about 1 hour.

Turn the dough out onto a lightly floured surface and roll out to a thickness of 2.5 mm/ ⅛ inch. Stamp out rounds using the larger cookie cutter and line the muffin pan with the dough. Bring any scraps of dough together, re-roll and stamp out as many rounds as you can. Chill in the fridge again for 30 minutes.

Preheat the oven to 160°C (325°F) Gas 3.

Line each round with foil or baking parchment and fill with baking beans or rice. Bake the rounds for 10 minutes, then remove the beans or rice and foil or parchment, and bake for a further 5 minutes. Cool in the pan.

To make the honey caramel, first soak the gelatin in cold water for 10 minutes. Put the honey in a pan set over a medium heat, leave it to melt, then turn up the heat and bring to the boil – be careful not to boil too much as you only want to caramelize it slightly.

In a second pan warm the cream, then carefully pour over the honey – it will bubble up a lot. Add the salt, bring back to the boil and remove from the heat. Add the butter and stir until melted. Drain the gelatin and squeeze off any excess water before adding to the caramel. Stir in, then pour into a jug/pitcher and set in the fridge to cool.

To build the tarts, pour the honey caramel two-thirds of the way up the cooled pastry cases. Set aside to cool completely.

Temper the chocolate by melting in the microwave in bursts of 30 seconds. Once the mixture is three-quarters melted, stop heating and stir well to remove any lumps. Spread the tempered chocolate thinly on the cocoa butter transfer sheet with the printed cocoa butter pattern facing up. Leave to cool slightly and just as it starts to set, use the smaller cookie cutter to stamp out rounds of the chocolate. Leave to cool completely before removing and fitting snuggly on top of the tarts.

Pipe a small dot of lemon curd and a beehive shape on each tart and carefully fix a sugar bee to the dots.

One of the first things I learnt to make at school in Food Technology class was jam tarts. I've used Breton pastry which is aerated so gives you a wonderfully light and rich texture and filled with them different homemade fillings; here, strawberry jam/jelly, marmalade and lemon curd – delightful.

Jam tarts

150 g/1 stick plus
    2 tablespoons butter,
    softened
100 g/½ cup caster/
    granulated sugar
3 egg yolks
200 g/1⅔ cups plain/
    all-purpose flour
½ teaspoon baking
    powder
a pinch of salt
zest of 1 lemon
zest of 1 orange
8 tablespoons good-
    quality jams and curds
    of your choosing
    (pages 11–15)

*a 6–7-cm/2–3-inch fluted
round cookie cutter
2 x 12-hole muffin pans,
greased*

Makes 24

Combine the butter with the sugar in the bowl of a stand mixer and beat until pale and light – this will take about 5 minutes.

Gradually add the egg yolks one at a time and mix until they are thoroughly combined. Sift the flour and baking powder into the bowl. Add the salt and grated citrus zest and fold in using a rubber spatula or large metal spoon. The dough will be soft and buttery.

Gather the dough together, form a ball and flatten into a disc. Cover with clingfilm/plastic wrap and chill in the fridge for at least 2 hours until firm.

Preheat the oven to 180°C (350°F) Gas 4.

Roll out the dough on a lightly floured work surface to a thickness of 2 mm/1/16 inch. Using the cutter, stamp out discs from the dough and gently press into the prepared muffin pans.

Drop a teaspoonful of jam or curd into each tart and bake on the middle shelf of the preheated oven for about 12 minutes until the pastry is golden brown and the jam/jelly is bubbling.

Leave to cool for a few minutes before transferring to a wire rack to cool completely – the jam/jelly and curd needs to set before serving.

These really are a little tangy sensation! A crisp pastry flavoured with freeze-dried passionfruit powder filled with a tangy passionfruit curd and topped with Italian meringue, flamed with a blowtorch to add a little caramelized flavour. For afternoon tea, little ones are perfect, but if you were entertaining for larger numbers, a large tart would go down a treat!

Passionfruit meringue tarts

100 g/6½ tablespoons butter, softened
50 g/⅓ cup icing/confectioners' sugar
a pinch of salt
1 egg, lightly beaten
1 teaspoon vanilla bean paste
175 g/1⅓ cups plain/all-purpose flour
1 tablespoon freeze-dried passionfruit powder
passionfruit curd (page 12), for the filling

MERINGUE
125 g/scant ⅔ cup caster/superfine sugar
2 egg whites, at room temperature
a pinch of cream of tartar
a pinch of salt

a 8–9-cm/3–3½-inch round cookie cutter
12 x 7-cm/5 x 3-inch shallow mini tart pans
baking beans (optional)
a sugar thermometer
a disposable piping/pastry bag (optional)
a blow torch

Makes 12

Cream the butter, icing/confectioners' sugar and salt together in a stand mixer or in a large mixing bowl with a handheld electric whisk until pale – this will take 3–4 minutes.

With the mixer running, gradually add the beaten egg with the vanilla bean paste, mixing until fully incorporated. Gently mix in the flour and passionfruit powder but do not overwork the dough. Bring the dough together into a ball, wrap in clingfilm/plastic wrap, flatten into a disc and chill in the fridge for at least 2 hours or until needed.

Roll out the dough on a lightly floured work surface to an even thickness of no more than 2 mm/¹⁄₁₆ inch. Stamp out discs using the cookie cutter. Neatly line the tart pans with the discs and trim off any excess from the top with a small sharp knife. Prick the bases with a fork, line with a square of foil or baking parchment and fill with baking beans or rice. Arrange the pans on a baking sheet and chill in the fridge for 20 minutes.

Preheat the oven to 180°C (350°F) Gas 4.

Bake on the middle shelf of the oven for 10–12 minutes or until pale golden. Remove the beans or rice and foil and baking parchment and continue to cook for 1 minute until the bases are crisp. Remove from the oven and set aside to cool.

Divide the passionfruit curd between the baked tart shells and chill for 20 minutes while you prepare the meringue.

To make the meringue, tip the caster/superfine sugar into a small pan and add 75 ml/5 tablespoons of water. Set the pan over a low heat. Once the sugar is dissolved, bring to the boil and pop a sugar thermometer into the pan.

Meanwhile, tip the egg whites into the bowl of a stand mixer fitted with a whisk attachment and add the cream of tartar and salt.

Continue to cook the syrup until it reaches 110°C (230°F) on the thermometer. Then start whisking the egg whites until they will hold soft, floppy peaks. Remove the syrup from the heat, and with the mixer running on a medium speed, steadily pour into the egg whites being careful to not let the syrup hit the whisk, otherwise it will simply splatter against the sides of the bowl. Increase the speed and continue whisking for a further 4–5 minutes until the meringue is cool, stiff and glossy. Working quickly either spoon the meringue on top of the passionfruit tarts or fill a piping/pastry bag and pipe peaks on top.

Light the blow torch and lightly scorch the meringue. Leave to cool before serving.

Lemon drizzle cake is one of the UK's favourite cakes; soft and buttery sponge spiked with lemon and finished with a lemon sugar that sometimes makes you feel like you've had teaspoon of lemon sherbet. Here, I've based madeleines on the classic lemon drizzle but using polenta that gives a lovely texture. Finish with a lemon sugar glaze or you could even add some fresh rosemary for a fragrant twist.

Lemon and polenta drizzle cakes

150 g/1 stick plus
2 tablespoons butter, melted
125 g/1 cup plain/ all-purpose flour, plus extra for dusting
1½ teaspoons baking powder
50 g/⅓ cup polenta/cornmeal
a pinch of salt
2 eggs, beaten
125 g/scant ⅔ cup caster/superfine sugar
zest of ½ lemon and juice of 2
3 tablespoons granulated/white sugar

a 12-hole madeleine pan

Makes 12

Brush melted butter on the inside of the madeleine pan moulds so that they are thoroughly and well greased. Dust the pans with a little flour and tip out any excess. Chill in the fridge for 15 minutes.

Sift the flour and baking powder into a large mixing bowl. Add the polenta/cornmeal and the salt, mix together and set aside.

In a separate bowl, whisk the beaten eggs with the caster/superfine sugar for about 5 minutes until the mixture has thickened and doubled in volume – this can be done either in a stand mixer or using a handheld electric whisk. Add the lemon zest and one-quarter of the juice to the mixture.

Using a large metal spoon, fold the sifted dry ingredients into the egg mixture in a figure of '8' action. Carefully pour the remaining melted butter around the edge of the mixture and fold in.

Cover the bowl and chill in the fridge for 30 minutes while you preheat the oven to 190°C (375°F) Gas 5.

Divide the batter between the holes in the chilled pan and bake on the middle shelf of the preheated oven for about 12–14 minutes until well risen and golden. Remove from the oven and cool in the pan for 2 minutes, then carefully turn out onto a wire rack suspended over a baking sheet or piece of baking parchment.

Add the granulated/white sugar to the remaining lemon juice and mix to combine, but do not allow the sugar to dissolve. Spoon the lemony sugar mix slowly over the top of the warm madeleines – the baking sheet or parchment will catch any drips.

Leave until completely cold before serving. Madeleines are best eaten on the day that they are made.

Carrot cake

100 g/⅔ cup (dark)
    raisins
zest and juice of
    1 orange
100 g/¾ cup blanched
    hazelnuts or walnuts
350 g/2½ cups grated
    carrot
75 g/1 cup desiccated/
    shredded coconut
250 ml/1 cup sunflower
    or groundnut (peanut)
    oil
125 ml/½ cup hazelnut
    or walnut oil
400 g/2 cups caster/
    granulated sugar
3 eggs plus 2 egg whites
375 g/3 cups plain/
    all-purpose flour
2 teaspoons baking
    powder
1 teaspoon bicarbonate
    of soda/baking soda
1 teaspoon ground
    cinnamon
a pinch of salt

TOPPING
75 g/½ cup blanched
    hazelnuts
600 g/20 oz. cream
    cheese
4 tablespoons clear
    honey, maple or agave
    syrup

*2 x 450-g/1-lb. capacity
loaf pans or 3 x 20-cm/
8-inch sandwich pans,
greased and base-lined
with baking parchment
a disposable piping/
pastry bag*

Serves 8–10

During the Second World War, sugar was rationed and expensive. Carrots are the sweetest of vegetables apart from sugar beet, so people would grow carrots in their gardens and use them in cakes. I've added hazelnut oil and a little meringue to lighten the cake and also add to the nutty flavour that I really like.

Tip the raisins into a bowl and add half the orange zest and juice, stir to combine, then cover and set aside for about 4 hours or preferably overnight for the raisins to absorb the orange juice and become plump.

Preheat the oven to 170°C (325°F) Gas 3.

Finely chop the hazelnuts or walnuts and add to the soaked raisins with the grated carrot and desiccated/shredded coconut. Mix well to combine.

In another bowl combine the hazelnut or walnut oil with 250 g/1¼ cups of the sugar and 3 whole eggs, and whisk for about 2 minutes until thoroughly combined and foamy. Add the carrot mixture to the bowl and fold in with a metal spoon.

In another bowl, whisk the remaining 2 egg whites with the remaining 125 g/¾ cup sugar and the salt until stiff and glossy.

Sift the dry ingredients into the carrot mixture and fold in using a large metal spoon. Add a large spoonful of the meringue and fold in to lighten the batter slightly. Add the remaining meringue and gently fold in. Divide the batter between the prepared

pans, spread level and bake on the middle shelf of the preheated oven for 40–45 minutes or until a skewer inserted into the middle of the cakes comes out clean.

Leave the cakes to cool in the pans for 5 minutes, then turn out onto a wire rack and leave until completely cold.

While the oven is still on toast the hazelnuts for the topping. Tip the nuts onto a baking sheet and toast in the oven for 4–5 minutes. Leave to cool, then roughly chop.

Scoop the cream cheese into a bowl, add the remaining orange zest and juice, honey, maple or agave syrup and beat well to thoroughly combine. Transfer to the piping/pastry bag and set in the fridge if the cakes aren't completely cold yet.

Pipe bulbs of the cream onto each loaf or lay one of the cake layers on the serving plate and spread or pipe with one-third of the topping. Cover with the second cake layer and pipe on another third of the topping. Place the final cake on top and pipe the remaining topping on.

Scatter with the hazelnuts and serve in slices.

Mini mocha cakes

150 g/1 cup plus 2 tablespoons plain/all-purpose flour

125 g/scant ⅔ cup caster/granulated sugar

100 g/½ cup soft light brown sugar

40 g/¼ cup cocoa powder, plus extra for dusting

1 teaspoon baking powder

½ teaspoon bicarbonate of soda/baking soda

a pinch of salt, plus extra to taste

100 g/⅓ cup whole milk

75 ml/scant ⅓ cup sunflower oil

1 egg, lightly beaten

1 teaspoon vanilla extract

100 ml/⅓ cup hot coffee

MERINGUE BUTTERCREAM

175 g/¾ cup plus 2 tablespoons golden caster/raw cane sugar

3 egg whites

200 g/1¾ sticks butter, softened

3 teaspoons instant coffee granules

2 x 12-hole mini muffin pans base-lined with baking parchment and greased

a sugar thermometer

a large piping/pastry bag fitted with a star nozzle/tip

Makes 24

These delightful chocolate cakes are filled and topped with coffee-flavoured meringue buttercream and are a lovely way of serving cake at afternoon tea parties. It's good to serve big cakes, too, of course, but sometimes it's extra special to have a mini individual cake all to yourself!

Preheat the oven to 180°C (350°F) Gas 4.

Sift the flour, cocoa powder, baking powder, bicarbonate of soda/baking soda into the bowl of a stand mixer fitted with a whisk attachment or into a large mixing bowl with a handheld electric whisk. Add the caster/granulated and soft light brown sugars and a pinch of salt. Make a well in the middle and add the milk, sunflower oil, beaten egg and vanilla extract. Add the hot coffee and beat well for about 2 minutes until smooth. As the batter is wet you will find it easier to pour it into a jug/pitcher to divide it between the paper cases rather than using a spoon or ladle. Fill each hole in the pan to within 2 mm/¹⁄₁₆ inch from the top.

Bake on the middle shelf of the preheated oven for about 20 minutes or until well risen and a skewer inserted into the middle of the cakes comes out clean. Leave the cakes to cool in the pans for 2 minutes, then transfer to a wire rack until completely cold.

To make the meringue frosting, combine 25 g/2 tablespoons of the golden caster/raw cane sugar with the egg whites in the bowl of a stand mixer fitted with a whisk attachment. Tip the remaining sugar into a small pan, add 75 ml/5 tablespoons of water and set over a low–medium heat to dissolve the sugar. Bring to the boil and continue to cook until the syrup reaches 118°C (244°F) on a sugar thermometer.

Remove the pan from the heat and working quickly whisk the egg whites at fast speed until they will hold a just firm peak. Slowly and steadily, with the motor running on a low speed, pour the hot syrup into the mixer. Increase the speed and continue whisking until the mixture has become cold and is whipped into glossy peaks. Dissolve the coffee in 3 teaspoons of boiling water and add to the meringue. Gradually add the butter beating well between each addition. Spoon the meringue buttercream into the large piping/pastry bag.

Remove the cakes from the pans and discard the baking parchment if it sticks to the bottom. Slice the cakes in half, pipe a small amount of meringue buttercream on the base, top with the other half and pipe a swirl on top of each cake. Dust with cocoa powder to serve.

Fruit cake *with an orange glaze*

150 g/1 cup mixed dried
  fruit
100 g/2/3 cup chopped
  dried apricots
40 g/1/3 cup chopped
  mixed candied peel
100 g/3/4 cup glacé
  cherries, rinsed and
  quartered
2 nuggets of stem ginger
  in syrup, drained and
  finely chopped
zest and juice of 1 orange
1 tablespoon brandy
175 g/1½ sticks butter
75 g/1/3 cup light
  muscovado sugar
75 g/1/3 cup caster/
  granulated sugar
3 eggs, beaten
1 tablespoon golden
  syrup/light corn syrup
1 tablespoon treacle/dark
  molasses
200 g/1²/3 cups plain/
  all-purpose flour
1 teaspoon baking powder
1 teaspoon ground
  mixed spice/apple
  pie spice
a pinch of salt
1 rounded tablespoon
  demerara/turbinado
  sugar

ORANGE GLAZE
zest and juice of 1 orange
100 g/3/4 cup icing/
  confectioners' sugar

*a 900-g/2-lb. loaf pan or
4 x mini loaf pans, base
and ends lined with
buttered baking parchment*

Serves 12

My Nans always used to make fruit cake topped with marzipan and icing for our childhood birthdays. Although it wasn't my favourite back then, I have grown to love a good fruit cake. I like to make two different types; this one, a little lighter finished with an orange glaze and, of course, one at Christmas with more fruit (and more booze) finished with a brandy glacé icing.

Tip the dried fruit, apricots, candied peel, glacé cherries and stem ginger into a small pan. Add the orange zest, juice and brandy, and heat gently for 1 minute until the juice is hot but not boiling. Remove from the heat and leave to cool for about 1 hour for the fruit to plump up and absorb the liquid.

Preheat the oven to 170°C (325°F) Gas 3.

Cream together the butter, light muscovado and caster/granulated sugar until pale and light, this will take about 3 minutes in a stand mixer. Gradually add the beaten eggs mixing well between each addition and scraping down the sides of the bowl with a rubber spatula from time to time. Add the golden syrup/light corn syrup and treacle/dark molasses and mix again until combined.

Sift the flour, baking powder, mixed spice/apple pie spice and salt into the bowl and fold in using a rubber spatula or large metal spoon. Add the dried fruit mixture and mix again to thoroughly combine.

Spoon the cake batter into the prepared loaf pan or pans, scatter with demerara/turbinado sugar and bake just below the middle of the oven for about 25 minutes. Reduce the heat to 160°C (300°F) Gas 2 and continue to cook for a further 1 hour or until well risen, golden brown and a skewer inserted into the middle of the cake comes out clean.

Leave to rest in the pan for 2–3 minutes, then slide a palette knife down the sides to loosen and carefully turn the cake out onto a wire rack. Leave until completely cold.

Meanwhile make the orange glaze by mixing the orange zest and juice with the icing/confectioners' sugar, adding just enough water to make a thin paste. Drizzle over the cake while still warm and leave to set.

This cake is best made a day ahead as it is easier to slice.

Pulled ham hock sandwiches
with piccalilli mayonnaise

'Coronation' chicken sandwiches
with pickled red onion

Crab mayonnaise éclairs

St Clement's posset *with basil sablés*

Prosecco, lime and mint jellies

Passionfruit 'jaffa' cakes

Chocolate and cherry tarts

Strawberries and cream cakes

The Berkeley Pistachio and
strawberry délices

Mango and coconut millefeuilles

Rum savarin *with charred
pineapple and coconut Chantilly*

Marmalade Madeira cakes *with macadamias,
hazelnuts and almonds*

Caramelized pineapple 'upside down' cakes

Summer
sensation

Ham and piccalilli sandwiches are a must have for a quintessentially British picnic and here I've used pulled/shredded ham hock which is now readily available in supermarkets and blended piccalilli with mayonnaise for an afternoon tea twist. The addition of some thinly sliced, lightly pickled cauliflower really adds flavour and of course texture. If you can't find pulled/shredded ham hock, you can use good-quality wafer thin sliced ham.

Pulled ham hock sandwiches
with piccalilli mayonnaise

½ small cauliflower
4 tablespoons white wine or cider vinegar
4 tablespoons piccalilli
2 tablespoons mayonnaise
10 slices white bread
75 g/5 tablespoons salted butter, softened
250 g/2 cups pulled/shredded ham hock (or 20 slices/8 oz. good-quality wafer thin/sliced ham)
a good handful of watercress or wild rocket/arugula
salt and freshly ground black pepper, to taste

Makes 20

First prepare the cauliflower. Trim the leaves from the cauliflower but leave the stalk intact. Very finely slice it, using either a long, sharp knife or mandoline slicer if you have one. Tip the slices into a bowl, add the vinegar, season with salt and black pepper and toss gently to coat. Set aside at room temperature for at least 1 hour and up to 4 hours to pickle.

Tip the piccalilli into a food processor and pulse until the vegetables are finely chopped but stop before they are reduced to a purée. Spoon into a bowl, add the mayonnaise and mix to combine.

Lay the bread slices out on the work surface and lightly spread with butter. Season with salt and black pepper. Spread half of the bread slices with piccalilli mayonnaise and top with the pulled/shredded ham. Drain the cauliflower slices from the vinegar and lay on top of the ham. Arrange some watercress or wild rocket/arugula leaves on top of the cauliflower and top with the remaining bread slices, butter side down.

Gently press the sandwiches together, slice off the crusts and cut into delicate triangles. Arrange on a plate and serve immediately.

'Coronation' chicken sandwiches
with pickled red onion

1 red onion
2 tablespoons cider or white wine vinegar
1 teaspoon golden caster/raw cane sugar
100 ml/⅓ cup whipping cream
150 g/¾ cup full-fat Greek yogurt
1–2 tablespoons ready-made tikka curry paste
1 teaspoon medium curry powder
3 tablespoons mango chutney
juice of ½ lime
3 cooked chicken breasts
75 g/½ cup sultanas/ golden raisins
1 teaspoon nigella or kalonji/black onion seeds
8 slices white bread
150 g/1 stick plus 2 tablespoons butter, softened
a handful of fresh coriander/cilantro leaves
salt and freshly ground black pepper, to taste

Makes 24

Coronation chicken was invented to celebrate the coronation of Queen Elizabeth II in 1953 and to update it I've used tikka curry paste to form the base of my filling and added pickled red onion, fresh coriander/cilantro and black onion seeds for a curry twist. You could go one step further and serve them in mini naan breads. I like to soak the sultanas/golden raisins in lager for an hour or so before using them to add another level of flavour.

Start by lightly pickling the red onion. Peel, half and thinly slice the onion and tip into a bowl. Add the vinegar, sugar and a pinch of salt. Mix well, cover and set aside for 1 hour to allow the onion slices to soften.

In another bowl lightly whip the cream so that it will barely hold a peak. Add the Greek yogurt, tikka curry paste, curry powder, half of the mango chutney and the lime juice. Season with salt and black pepper and mix gently to combine.

Shred the chicken breasts and add to the curried yogurt along with the sultanas/golden raisins (drained of any excess liquid if you have hydrated them in lager as per the introduction above) and the nigella or kalonji/black onion seeds. Mix to coat the chicken.

Drain the red onion from the pickling liquid.

Lay the bread slices out on the work surface and spread with a thin layer of butter, followed by a layer of reserved mango chutney. Divide the chicken mixture between half of the bread slices and top with a pinch of pickled red onion slices. Scatter with fresh coriander/cilantro leaves and top with the remaining bread slices.

Gently press the sandwiches together and cut into fingers or triangles to serve.

Crab mayonnaise éclairs

75 ml/5 tablespoons
   whole milk
60 g/4 tablespoons
   butter
100 g/¾ cup plain/
   all-purpose flour
a good pinch of cayenne
   pepper
a good pinch of dry
   mustard powder
3 eggs, lightly beaten
1–2 tablespoons finely
   grated Parmesan
   cheese
wild rocket/arugula,
   mizuna or baby leaf
   spinach leaves
salt and freshly ground
   black pepper, to taste

CRAB MAYONNAISE
4 tablespoons good-
   quality mayonnaise
zest and juice of ½
   lemon
½–1 teaspoon Dijon
   mustard
a pinch of cayenne
   pepper
250 g/8 oz. white crab
   meat

*a large piping/pastry bag
fitted with a 1-cm/⅜-inch
plain nozzle/tip
2 baking sheets lined
with baking parchment*

Makes about 30

These savoury spiced éclairs simply encase beautifully picked white crab meat, with a little lemon and mustard mayonnaise finished off with some peppery rocket/arugula. They go perfectly with chilled Champagne or for a dinner party tea service, an espresso cup of crab or lobster bisque.

Preheat the oven to 180°C (350°F) Gas 4.

Put 75 ml/5 tablespoons of water in a medium pan with the milk and butter and set over a medium heat. Stir constantly to melt the butter. As soon as the mixture comes to the boil, reduce the heat slightly and, working quickly and keeping the pan over a low heat, stir in the flour, cayenne pepper and mustard powder. Season well with salt and black pepper. Beat vigorously until the mixture is smooth and cleanly leaves the sides of the pan – this will take about 2 minutes.

Transfer the dough to a stand mixer or mixing bowl using a handheld electric whisk and gradually beat in the eggs 1 tablespoon at a time. You might not need all of the egg – when the dough is soft and smooth and drops off a spoon leaving a 'V' shape behind it is ready.

Scoop the dough into the piping/pastry bag and pipe 30 éclair buns onto the prepared baking sheets leaving plenty of space between each one. Scatter with grated Parmesan cheese and bake on the middle shelves of the preheated oven for 10–15 minutes until well risen, golden brown and sound hollow in the middle when tapped.

Remove from the oven and make a small hole in the side of each bun with a skewer. Return to the oven for a further 1 minute to dry out the insides. Leave to cool on a wire rack until completely cold.

To make the crab mayonnaise, spoon the mayonnaise into a bowl, add the lemon zest and juice, mustard, cayenne pepper and a good seasoning of salt and black pepper. Mix to combine and taste. Add more salt and black pepper if required, then add the crab meat and stir gently to coat.

Using a serrated knife split the éclairs in half, lay wild rocket/arugula, mizuna or baby spinach leaves in the bottom of each bun and top with a heaped teaspoonful of crab mayonnaise. Put the lids on and serve.

The simplicity of the classic lemon posset makes it one of my all time favourite desserts. Just three ingredients; lemon, cream and sugar. The addition of orange for my take, makes this posset really summery. Serve with a crumbly basil sablé to dip in. Basil, lemon and orange is a fantastic flavour combination – you could even try serving the posset with a strawberry and basil or raspberry and mint salad.

St Clement's posset *with basil sablés*

**zest and juice of
  2 lemons and 1 orange**
**500 ml/2 cups double/
  heavy cream**
**100 g/½ cup caster/
  granulated sugar**

BASIL SABLÉS
**75 g/5 tablespoons
  butter, softened**
**40 g/¼ cup icing/
  confectioners' sugar**
**seeds from ½ vanilla
  pod/bean**
1 teaspoon lemon zest
1 egg, lightly beaten
**a small bunch of fresh
  basil, finely chopped**
**125 g/1 cup plain/
  all-purpose flour**
a pinch of salt

TO SERVE (OPTIONAL)
thin segments of orange
tiny basil leaves
a few drops of orange oil

*12 serving glasses
a 3–4-cm/1¼–1½-inch
round cookie cutter
a baking sheet lined
with baking parchment*

Serves 12

Tip the citrus zest into a pan and set over a low–medium heat. Pour the cream into the pan, add the caster/granulated sugar and bring slowly to the boil, stirring to dissolve the sugar.

Slide the pan off the heat and add the citrus juices. Whisk quickly to combine, then pass the mixture through a fine mesh sieve/strainer into a jug/pitcher before carefully pouring into serving glasses. Leave to cool, then cover and chill in the fridge for at least 4 hours until set.

While the possets are setting prepare the basil sablés. Cream the butter and icing/confectioners' sugar together until pale and light. Add the vanilla seeds and lemon zest and mix to combine. Gradually add the beaten egg, mixing well between each addition. Add the chopped basil and mix gently to combine. Sift the flour into the bowl and add the salt. Fold in using a large metal spoon or rubber spatula. Gather the dough into a smooth ball, flatten into a disc, wrap in clingfilm/plastic wrap and chill in the fridge for 1 hour.

Preheat the oven to 170°C (325°F) Gas 3.

Roll out the dough on a lightly floured work surface to a thickness of no more than 2 mm/1/16 inch. Cut out small rounds using the cookie cutter and arrange on the prepared baking sheet. Bring the scraps together, re-roll and stamp out as many as you can.

Bake on the middle shelf of the preheated oven for 8–10 minutes until firm and golden.

Cool on a wire rack until cold, then store in an airtight container until ready to serve alongside the posset.

What could be better to celebrate with than jelly! I used to love jelly and ice cream as a child at my birthday parties but this is one for the adults. The key to keeping the bubbles is to give the mixture a quick whisk before you pour it into the glasses. The lime and mint foam on top really excites the palette, too!

Prosecco, lime and mint jellies

100 g/½ cup caster/
   granulated sugar
2 large sprigs fresh mint
peel of 2 limes
7 sheets platinum-grade
   leaf gelatin
a 750-ml bottle Prosecco,
   lightly chilled

LIME AND MINT FOAM
juice of 2 limes
75 g/5 tablespoons
   caster/superfine sugar
2 sprigs fresh mint
2 sheets platinum-grade
   leaf gelatin

*a 1-litre/quart capacity
jug/pitcher*

Serves 6–8

Start by making a lime and mint infusion. Tip the caster/granulated sugar into a small pan, add the fresh mint and lime peel. Add 100 ml/⅓ cup of water and set the pan over a low heat to dissolve the sugar. Bring to the boil, reduce to a gentle simmer and continue to cook for 1 minute. Remove from the heat and leave to cool and infuse at room temperature for at least 2 hours.

Soak the gelatin leaves in a large bowl of cold water for 10 minutes until softened. Strain the lime and mint infusion through a fine mesh sieve/strainer into a clean pan. Bring back to the boil, then immediately remove from the heat. Squeeze out any excess water from the gelatin and add to the hot syrup. Stir until melted and smooth.

Carefully open the bottle of Prosecco. Pour the gelatin mixture into the large measuring jug/pitcher and very slowly, pouring down the inside of the jug/pitcher, add one-quarter of the Prosecco. Mix to combine, then slowly (to prevent it fizzing up) add the remaining Prosecco. Stir gently to combine and then carefully pour the jelly mixture into small glasses or ideally Champagne flutes. Arrange on a tray and chill in the fridge for at least 4 hours until set.

To make the lime and mint foam pour the lime juice into a small pan along with the caster/superfine sugar and mint sprigs. Set the pan over a low heat to dissolve the sugar, bring to the boil, simmer for 30 seconds, then remove from the heat. Cool at room temperature for 1 hour to allow the mint to infuse with the syrup.

Soak the gelatin leaves in a bowl of cold water for 10 minutes until softened. Bring the syrup back to the boil, remove from the heat, strain into a clean jug/pitcher and make the liquid up to 200 ml/¾ cup with extra water.

Squeeze out any excess water from the gelatin and add to the hot syrup. Stir until melted. Leave to cool completely or stand the jug/pitcher in a bowl of ice-cold water and, using a bar mixer or hand whisk, beat the syrup furiously until it cools and foams up into clouds of minty lime bubbles.

Spoon a little foam on top of each jelly and return to the fridge to set for about 1 hour before serving.

Who else eats the jelly first, then the sponge? Or is that just me? Either way, I love a jaffa cake and my version is made with a passionfruit and orange jelly dipped in rich dark/bittersweet chocolate that balances really well.

Passionfruit 'jaffa' cakes

JELLY/GELATIN LAYER

4 sheets platinum-grade leaf gelatin

7 passionfruit

250 ml/1 cup orange juice

1–2 tablespoons caster/ superfine sugar

CAKE LAYER

100 g/6½ tablespoons butter, softened

75 g/5 tablespoons caster/granulated sugar

2 eggs, lightly beaten

1 teaspoon vanilla extract

125 g/1 cup plain/ all-purpose flour

½ teaspoon baking powder

a pinch of salt

TO FINISH

200 g/6½ oz. dark/ bittersweet chocolate, chopped

a 20 x 30-cm/8 x 12-inch baking sheet, oiled and lined with clingfilm/ plastic wrap

2 x 12-hole muffin pans, greased and holes base-lined with baking parchment

a 5-cm/2-inch round cookie cutter

Makes 18–20

First, prepare the jelly/gelatin layer. Soak the gelatin leaves in cold water for 10 minutes until softened. Cut the passionfruit in half and scoop the juice, pulp and seeds into a small pan. Add the orange juice and bring to the boil over a low heat. Remove from the heat and pass through a fine mesh sieve/ strainer into a bowl, pushing the passionfruit seeds to extract as much juice and pulp as possible. Add caster/superfine sugar to taste. Squeeze out any excess water from the gelatin and blot with paper towels. Add to the orange juice, whisk to melt, then pour onto the prepared baking sheet. Cool at room temperature, then cover and chill for at least 4 hours or overnight until set firm.

Preheat the oven to 170°C (325°F) Gas 3.

Cream the butter with the caster/granulated sugar until light and fluffy. Gradually add the beaten eggs, mixing well between each addition. Add the vanilla extract and mix again. Sift the flour, baking powder, and salt into the bowl and mix until smooth.

Divide the mixture between the prepared muffin pans – each hole should have 1 heaped teaspoon of mixture. Spread the mixture level in the pans with the back of a teaspoon and bake on the middle shelf of the preheated oven for 10–12 minutes until pale golden at the edges.

Run a palette knife around the edge of each cake to release it and cool on a wire rack. Peel off the baking parchment if it sticks to the underside of the cakes. Turn the cakes the right side up and leave until cold. Using a small serrated knife cut off any peaky tops from the cakes – the baker's treat.

To build the jaffa cakes, first temper the chocolate by melting in the microwave in bursts of 30 seconds. Once the mixture is three-quarters melted, stop heating and stir well to remove any lumps. Leave the chocolate to cool slightly before using – if it is too hot it will melt the passionfruit jelly/gelatin.

Lift the jelly/gelatin from the baking sheet, still on its clingfilm/plastic wrap, and place on the work surface. Using the cookie cutter stamp out as many discs from the jelly as you have cakes and using a palette knife carefully lift the discs, one at a time, onto a cake.

Arrange the jelly-topped cakes on a wire rack set over a sheet of baking parchment to catch any drips. Carefully spoon the tempered chocolate over the top and sides of each jaffa cake, tapping the wire rack to allow any excess chocolate to drip off. Leave to set for 10 minutes, then gently press the tines of a fork into the chocolate to make a ridge pattern. Set firm before serving.

Chocolate and cherry tarts

These tarts take their inspiration from the spiced, fruit-filled Austrian Linzertorte. My version sees hazelnut pastry cases filled with cherry compote and topped with hazelnut ganache. The tempered chocolate shards really help boost the chocolatey flavour and give extra crunch.

HAZELNUT PASTRY

150 g/1 cup plus 2 tablespoons plain/all-purpose flour

50 g/½ cup ground hazelnuts

½ teaspoon ground cinnamon

a pinch of salt

100 g/7 tablespoons butter, chilled and diced

25 g/1½ tablespoons icing/confectioners' sugar

1 egg, lightly beaten

HAZELNUT GANACHE

75 ml/scant ⅓ cup whipping cream

100 g/¾ cup chopped dark/bittersweet chocolate

75 g/generous ½ cup chopped milk/semi-sweet chocolate

20 g/1 tablespoon honey

50 g/3½ tablespoons hazelnut purée/butter

TO DECORATE

cherry compote (page 14)

200 g/1½ cup chopped dark/bittersweet chocolate

red lustre powder (optional)

12 fresh cherries

a 9–10-cm/3½–4-inch round cookie cutter

a 12-hole muffin pan, greased

baking beans (optional)

a disposable piping/pastry bag

Makes 12

Start by making the hazelnut pastry. Tip the flour and ground hazelnuts into the bowl of a food processor, add the cinnamon, salt and butter. Pulse to rub the butter into the flour until it is pale and sand-like in texture. Add the icing/confectioners' sugar and mix again to combine. Add the beaten egg and pulse until the mixture starts to come together. Tip the dough out onto the work surface and use your hands to bring it together to a neat ball. Flatten into a disc, cover in clingfilm/plastic wrap and chill in the fridge for at least 1 hour until firm.

Roll the dough out on a lightly floured work surface to a thickness of no more than 2 mm/1⁄16 inch. Using the cookie cutter stamp out 12 discs from the dough. Gently press the discs into the muffin pan, trying not to stretch the dough but making sure that the holes are evenly lined. Chill in the fridge for 20 minutes.

Preheat the oven to 170°C (350°F) Gas 5.

Line the tart cases with a square of baking parchment or foil and fill with baking beans or rice. Bake in the preheated oven for 10 minutes until pale golden and starting to crisp. Remove the tarts from the oven and carefully lift out the baking beans or rice and parchment or foil, and return the pans to the oven for 1 minute more to dry out the tart bases. Remove from the oven and leave until cold before removing from the pan.

Temper the chocolate for decorating by melting in the microwave in bursts of 30 seconds. Once the mixture is three-quarters melted, stop heating and stir well to remove any lumps. Spread out very thinly onto a sheet of baking parchment using a palette knife and set aside to harden. Once set, brush with red lustre powder.

Next, prepare the ganache. Tip all of the ganache ingredients into a heatproof bowl and set over a pan of barely simmering water. Stir gently to combine into a silky smooth mixture, remove from the heat and leave to cool for 15 minutes. Transfer to the piping/pastry bag and set aside.

To build the tarts, divide the cherry compote between the pastry cases and spread level. Pipe ganache over the cherry compote in an even, smooth layer. Finish each tart with a fresh cherry and crack the tempered chocolate to form shards that can be arranged on top. I find I often have a little dough leftover so I like to bake this with the tart cases and crumble it on top to serve.

Strawberries and cream cakes

100 g/6½ tablespoons butter, softened

75 g/⅓ cup clotted or double/heavy cream

175 g/¾ cup plus 2 tablespoons caster/granulated sugar

3 large eggs, beaten

½ teaspoon vanilla bean paste

175 g/1⅓ cups self-raising/rising flour

1 teaspoon baking powder

a pinch of salt

1 tablespoon whole milk

TO DECORATE

3 tablespoons Strawberry jam/jelly (page 11)

300 ml/1¼ cups double/heavy cream

1 tablespoon icing/confectioners' sugar

seeds from ½ vanilla pod/bean

300 g/3 cups strawberries, hulled and quartered

6 mini meringue shells

12 x mini loaf pans, a 12-hole loaf sheet or a 20 x 30-cm/8 x 12-inch rectangular cake pan, greased and lightly dusted with flour

a disposable piping/pastry bag

Makes 12

When it comes to summer berries, the champion has to be the beautiful strawberry. It takes its place in desserts like Eton Mess perfectly alongside whipped cream and meringue pieces and everyone loves it. So I thought how about having all of those components (with some clotted cream thrown in for good measure) in a cake and here we are!

Preheat the oven to 180°C (350°F) Gas 4.

Cream together the softened butter, clotted or double/heavy cream and caster/granulated sugar until really pale and fluffy, this will take about 3–5 minutes in a stand mixer and longer by hand. Gradually add the beaten eggs, mixing well between each addition. Add the vanilla bean paste and mix again until smooth.

Sift in the flour, baking powder and salt, and mix again until thoroughly combined. Add the milk and mix until smooth. Divide the batter evenly between the prepared loaf pans or large cake pan.

Arrange on a baking sheet (if using the loaf pans) and bake on the middle shelf of the preheated oven for 15 minutes until well risen, golden and a skewer inserted in the middle of the cakes comes out clean.

Cool in the pan or pans for 1–2 minutes, then turn out onto a wire rack to cool completely.

If using a large cake pan, first cut into fingers using a small serrated knife, then cut out a little rectangular hole from the top of each cake to make a well. Spoon 1 teaspoon of strawberry jam/jelly into each well.

Using a balloon whisk beat the double/heavy cream with the icing/confectioners' sugar and vanilla seeds until it will just hold a stiff peak. Spoon into the piping/pastry bag and pipe vanilla cream on top of each cake. Arrange the strawberries on top, lightly crush the meringues and scatter over the strawberries to serve.

Mourad Khiat, Head Pastry Chef of London's The Berkeley is known for creating the 'Prêt-à-Portea' afternoon tea. First launched in 2005, Mourad has worked alongside designers such as Alexander McQueen, Jimmy Choo, Anya Hindmarch, Burberry, Armani and more, taking inspiration from their designs to create exquisitely decorated pieces of pâtisserie. It has since been served to more than 400,000 guests and is world-renowned. The inspiration for these mini délices comes from the vivid colours of summer fashion lines.

Pistachio and strawberry délices

280 g/9½ oz. marzipan, softened
50 g/3½ tablespoons pistachio purée/paste
3 eggs, beaten
50 g/3½ tablespoons butter, melted
½ teaspoon grape seed oil
½ tablespoon Amaretto
15 g/1 tablespoon plain/all-purpose flour (T55)
15 g/1 tablespoon cornflour/cornstarch
a pinch of baking powder

WHIPPED GANACHE
115 ml/scant ½ cup whipping cream
12 g/1 tablespoon liquid glucose
150 g/5 oz. white chocolate, chopped

STRAWBERRY JELLY
625 g/22 oz. strawberry purée/paste
50 g/scant ¼ cup clear honey
18 g/1 heaped tablespoon yellow pectin
100 g/½ cup caster/granulated sugar
125 g/1¼ cups hulled strawberries, chopped

TO DECORATE (OPTIONAL)
gold leaf
caramelized pistachios (see method, page 33)

a 24-cm/9½-inch square baking pan, greased
a sugar thermometer
a piping/pastry bag fitted with a star nozzle/tip

Makes 32

First, make the whipped ganache. Gently melt the chocolate in a bowl suspended over a pan of barely simmering water. Remove from the heat when half melted. Pour the whipping cream and glucose into a pan. Bring to the boil, then immediately pour over the chocolate and stir to combine. Chill in the fridge overnight.

Preheat the oven to 180°C (350°F) Gas 4.

Beat the marzipan and the pistachio paste together in a large mixing bowl. Slowly add the beaten eggs a little at a time. Add the butter, grape seed oil and Amaretto, and mix well. Sift in the flour, cornflour/cornstarch and baking powder, and stir to combine. Pour the mixture into the prepared baking pan.

Bake in the preheated oven for 20 minutes, or until a skewer inserted into the middle of the cake comes out clean. Set aside.

To make the strawberry jelly, put the strawberry purée/paste and honey into a pan set over a medium heat. Mix the pectin and sugar together in a small bowl and, when the strawberry mixture reaches 45°C (113°F) using a sugar thermometer, add to the pan. Bring to the boil for about 3 minutes, then add the chopped strawberries and remove from the heat. While still warm, spread the jelly evenly over the top of the baked and cooled pistachio cake. Put in the fridge to set.

Whip the chilled ganache to a soft peak and put in the piping/pastry bag. Pipe it on top of the délice in small strips of the same size as you will cut the slices and set in the freezer for 3–4 hours.

Cut slices of about 3 x 6 cm/1¼ x 2½ inches. Decorate with gold leaf and caramelized pistachios, if desired, and serve.

Mango really benefits from a dressing of fresh lime juice and here I've paired it with a crème diplomat made with coconut milk for a tropical feel. With a brûléed top, the puff pastry layers have been baked between two baking sheets with icing/confectioners' sugar to caramelize to give you a level millefeuille.

Mango and coconut millefeuilles

375 g/13 oz. all-butter puff pastry/dough, thawed if frozen

100 g/⅔ cup icing/ confectioners' sugar

caster/granulated sugar, to sprinkle

COCONUT CRÈME DIPLOMAT

200 ml/¾ cup whole milk

150 ml/⅔ cup coconut milk

½ vanilla pod/bean

3 egg yolks

50 g/¼ cup caster/ superfine sugar

1½ tablespoons cornflour/cornstarch

1–2 tablespoons Malibu (optional)

250 ml/1 cup double/ heavy cream, whipped

MACERATED MANGO

1 large or 2 small ripe mangoes

zest and juice of 1 lime

2 baking sheets lined with baking parchment
1 baking sheet
a disposable piping/ pastry bag
a blow torch

Makes 12

Preheat the oven to 200°C (400°F) Gas 6.

Cut the pastry into three evenly sized pieces. Roll each piece out on a lightly floured work surface into neat 18 x 23-cm/7 x 9-inch rectangles. Lay clingfilm/plastic wrap on top of each rectangle and stack on top of a floured baking sheet. Chill the pastry in the fridge for 20 minutes until firm.

Transfer one of the rectangles to one of the lined baking sheets. Dust with icing/ confectioners' sugar and lay a sheet of baking parchment on top. Place an unlined baking sheet directly on top of the parchment and bake on the middle shelf of the preheated oven for about 12 minutes until the pastry is golden brown, crisp and caramelized on top. Bake the other pastry rectangles in the same way. Leave to cool, then, using a serrated knife, cut each rectangle into 7 x 4-cm/ 3 x 1½-inch rectangles – you need 36.

To make the coconut crème diplomat, heat the milk with the coconut milk and vanilla pod/bean in a small pan set over a low heat. Bring slowly just to the boil, then remove from the heat and leave to infuse for 15 minutes. Meanwhile beat the egg yolks with the caster/superfine sugar and cornflour/cornstarch until pale and light. Remove the vanilla pod/bean and reheat the vanilla-infused milk until just below boiling,

then, whisking constantly, pour into the bowl with the egg mixture. Mix until smooth, then return to the pan and, stirring constantly, heat over a low–medium heat until gently boiling and thickened. Add the Malibu, if using, and mix in. Strain the mixture through a fine mesh sieve/strainer into a bowl and cover the surface with clingfilm/plastic wrap to prevent a skin forming. Leave until cold, then fold the whipped cream through the mixture and scoop into the piping/pastry bag.

To prepare the mango, remove the skin using a sharp knife and cut the flesh into small dice. Discard the stone. Tip the flesh into a bowl, add the lime zest and juice, mix to combine and macerate for 30 minutes.

Lay 24 of the pastry rectangles on the work surface. Drain the mango from the lime juice. Pipe small bulbs of coconut crème diplomat at each corner of all 24 pastry rectangles. Place a few pieces of diced mango alongside the crème and continue piping crème alternated with mango until the surface of each rectangle is covered like a chequerboard.

Carefully place 12 garnished pastries on a serving plate and top with a second layer. Position the reserved pastry rectangles on top, sprinkle with caster/granulated sugar and flame lightly with a blow torch to brûlée the tops. Serve immediately.

Rum savarin *with charred pineapple and coconut Chantilly*

75 ml/5 tablespoons whole milk

150 g/1 cup plus 2 tablespoons strong white bread flour

2 teaspoons fast-action dried yeast

4 teaspoons caster/granulated sugar

a large pinch of salt

2 eggs, lightly beaten

75 g/5 tablespoons butter, melted and cooled

toasted coconut, to serve

WHITE CHOCOLATE AND COCONUT GANACHE
60 ml/¼ cup coconut milk

5 g/1 teaspoon liquid glucose

75 g/2½ oz. white chocolate, chopped

150 ml/⅔ cup whipping cream

LIME AND RUM SYRUP
zest and juice of 2 limes

400 g/2 cups caster/granulated sugar

3 tablespoons dark rum

CHARRED PINEAPPLE
½ ripe pineapple

3 tablespoons soft light brown sugar

1 tablespoon dark rum

zest and juice of 1 lime

a disposable piping/pastry bag (optional)

a 12-hole mini savarin pan, lightly greased

Makes 12

I love a savarin. Whether it's for afternoon tea or a dessert, the sweet dough soaked in dark rum and lime juice is just wonderful. Served here with a coconut and white chocolate Chantilly cream and charred pineapple, it's perfection on a small plate.

The night before you want to serve the savarins make the white chocolate and coconut ganache. Heat the coconut milk with the liquid glucose in a small pan over a medium heat until boiling. Tip the chopped white chocolate into a bowl, pour over the hot milk and stir gently to combine. Add the chilled whipping cream, mix to combine and chill for at least 2 hours until completely cold.

The next day, to make the savarins, warm the milk in a small pan over a low heat or in a heatproof jug/pitcher in the microwave until just hand hot. Mix the flour, yeast, sugar and salt together in a large mixing bowl and make a well in the middle. Add the warm milk and beaten eggs and mix well for 3–4 minutes to combine until the dough is silky smooth and elastic. Add the melted and cooled butter and mix in.

Pipe or spoon the dough into the prepared pan, cover loosely with clingfilm/plastic wrap and set aside in a warm place for 30–45 minutes until nearly doubled in size.

Meanwhile, prepare the lime and rum syrup. Put the lime zest and juice into a pan with the caster/granulated sugar and 500 ml/2 cups of water. Bring to the boil over a medium heat, then reduce to a gentle simmer for 5 minutes. Add the rum, remove from the heat but keep warm.

Preheat the oven to 200°C (400°F) Gas 6.

Bake the savarins on the middle shelf of the preheated oven for about 20 minutes or until golden brown and well-risen. Leave to cool in the pan for 2 minutes, then pop the savarins in the warm lime and rum syrup. Leave to soak in the syrup for about 5–10 minutes turning over to absorb the liquid equally on both sides – they should expand slightly.

Prepare the charred pineapple. Using a sharp knife remove the skin, any 'eyes' and the tough central core from the pineapple. Cut the flesh into wedges and tip into a shallow baking dish along with the soft brown sugar, rum, lime zest and juice. Toss to coat, cover and leave to marinade for 1 hour.

Preheat a ridged grill pan until smoking hot. Lift the pineapple from the marinade, allowing any excess liquid to drip back onto the dish before placing on the hot grill pan. Cook for about 1 minute on each side until tender and nicely charred. Remove from the pan and leave to cool before cutting into small pieces.

When ready to serve, top the savarins with a few pieces each of charred pineapple.

Whisk the ganache until it will hold soft peaks, then spoon into the middle of each savarin. Sprinkle with toasted coconut and serve.

Marmalade Madeira cakes *with macadamias, hazelnuts and almonds*

250 g/2 sticks butter, softened
250 g/1⅓ cups golden caster/raw cane sugar, plus extra for sprinkling on top
5 eggs, lightly beaten
1 teaspoon vanilla extract
zest of ½ lemon
zest of ½ orange
275 g/2 cups plus 2 tablespoons self-raising/rising flour
½ teaspoon baking powder
40 g/scant ½ cup ground almonds
40 g/scant ½ cup ground hazelnuts
a pinch of salt
2 tablespoons whole milk

TO DECORATE
3–4 tablespoons marmalade
50 g/⅔ cup toasted macadamia nuts, chopped, to decorate

2 x 450-g/1-lb loaf pans with the bases and ends lined with a strip of buttered baking parchment

Serves 10–12

The humble Madeira cake has formed the basis of many a happy afternoon tea party and sometimes you just need a simple no-fuss cake. That said, my version is made with three types of nuts; roasted macadamias, ground hazelnuts and ground almonds, topped off with marmalade. You could have this cake for breakfast too if you like! A selection of cakes for breakfast, how marvellous!

Preheat the oven to 170°C (325°F) Gas 3.

Tip the butter into the bowl of a stand mixer fitted with a creamer attachment. Add the golden caster/raw cane sugar and beat for at least 3 minutes until the mixture is really pale and light. Gradually add the beaten eggs, mixing well between each addition and scraping down the sides of the bowl with a rubber spatula from time to time. Add the vanilla extract and the lemon and orange zest, and mix again.

Sift in the flour and baking powder, then add the ground almonds, ground hazelnuts, salt and milk, and fold in using a large metal spoon or rubber spatula until smooth and thoroughly combined.

Divide the mixture between the prepared loaf pans and spread level with either an offset palette knife or the back of a spoon. Sprinkle with extra golden caster/raw cane sugar and bake on the middle shelf of the preheated oven for about 50–55 minutes until golden brown, well risen and a skewer inserted into the middle of cakes comes out clean.

Rest in the pan for 3–5 minutes while you gently warm the marmalade either in a small pan over a low–medium heat or in the microwave in bursts of 30 seconds.

Turn the cakes out of the pans and onto a wire rack, brush the tops with melted marmalade, scatter with toasted macadamia nuts and leave until cold before serving in slices.

Caramelized pineapple 'upside down' cakes

50 g/⅓ cup hazelnuts, lightly toasted

75 g/generous ½ cup plain/all-purpose flour

1 teaspoon baking powder

a pinch of salt

150 g/1 stick plus 2 tablespoons butter, softened

100 g/½ cup caster/granulated sugar

3 eggs, lightly beaten

40 g/½ cup desiccated/shredded coconut

2 tablespoons buttermilk or sour cream

TOPPING

350 g/2½ cups diced fresh pineapple (about 1 pineapple)

4 tablespoons light brown sugar

4 tablespoons dark brown sugar

100 g/6½ tablespoons butter

4 tablespoons bourbon or dark rum

a good pinch of smoked sea salt flakes

a good pinch of lightly crushed pink peppercorns

½ teaspoon vanilla bean paste

zest of 1 lime, to decorate

a 12-hole muffin pan greased with butter

Makes 12

I have very fond memories of school dinners and pineapple upside down cake was on the menu nearly every week, with canned pineapple and glacé cherries on top. I've ditched the canned pineapple and caramelized some fresh pineapple with bourbon and pink peppercorns, and drizzled boozy spiced caramel on top with a grating of fresh lime zest to give these cakes a more grown-up appeal.

Preheat the oven to 180°C (350°F) Gas 4.

Prepare the topping first. Cut the pineapple into 1-cm/⅜-inch dice. Put both the light and dark brown sugars and the butter into a large frying pan/skillet. Set over a low heat to melt the butter and dissolve the sugars. Simmer for 30 seconds and remove half of the buttery caramel from the pan and set aside. Add the diced pineapple to the pan and cook over a medium heat until the pineapple is tender and just starting to caramelize. Add half of the bourbon or rum, the sea salt flakes, pink peppercorns and vanilla bean paste, and cook for a further 30 seconds. Divide the pineapple and pan juices between the buttered muffin holes and set aside to cool while you prepare the cake mixture.

Add the remaining bourbon or rum to the reserved caramel and set aside until the cakes are cooked and cooled.

Whizz the toasted hazelnuts in a food processor until very finely chopped. Add the flour, baking powder and salt, and whizz again until combined.

Cream the butter with the caster/granulated sugar until pale and light, scraping down the sides of the bowl with a rubber spatula from time to time. Gradually add the beaten eggs, mixing well between each addition.

Add the flour and hazelnut mixture along with the desiccated/shredded coconut and buttermilk or sour cream, and mix again until thoroughly combined.

Divide the cake batter between the muffin holes and bake on the middle shelf of the preheated oven for about 20 minutes until well-risen, golden brown and a skewer inserted into the middle of the cakes comes out with a moist crumb attached.

Run a palette knife around the inside edge of each cake to release it from the pan and turn the pan upside down onto a baking sheet to release the cakes. Leave the cakes to cool to room temperature.

Heat the reserved rum caramel in a small pan over a low heat and spoon over the top of the cakes. Sprinkle with lime zest to serve.

Triple cheese scones
with whipped mustard butter

Pastrami and emmental open
sandwich *with thousand-
island coleslaw on brown rye*

Red wine poached pear,
Stilton and endive
on walnut bread

Eccles cakes *with Pedro
Ximénez and Manchego cheese*

Triple chocolate cookies

PBJ cookie sandwiches

Malty egg custard tarts

Pumpkin and pecan pies

Spiced pumpkin apple cakes

Vanilla and chocolate
Battenberg

Jam and coconut cakes

Black Forest fondant fancies

Gramercy Tavern
Mom's sour cherry cake

Coffee, walnut and
cardamom cake

Fall delights

Triple cheese scones *with whipped mustard butter*

350 g/2¾ cups plain/
all-purpose flour
100 g/¾ cup spelt flour
3 teaspoons baking
powder
½ rounded teaspoon
English mustard
powder
¼–½ teaspoon cayenne
pepper
75 g/5 tablespoons
butter, chilled and
diced
50 g/½ cup coarsely
grated Cheddar, plus
extra for the topping
50 g/½ cup coarsely
grated Gruyère
25 g/⅓ cup finely grated
Parmesan, plus extra
for the topping
125 ml/½ cup buttermilk
150 ml/⅔ cup whole
milk, plus 1 tablespoon
for glazing
salt and freshly ground
black pepper, to taste

MUSTARD BUTTER
125 g/1 stick butter,
softened
1 teaspoon English
mustard
1 teaspoon grainy
mustard
2 teaspoons finely
chopped fresh chives

*a 5-cm/2-inch round
cookie cutter
a baking sheet lined
with baking parchment*

Makes about 18

Another of my Nans' favourite recipes was her cheese scones, fresh out of the oven and spread with butter that melted instantly. In my version I've added three different cheeses; Cheddar, Gruyère and Parmesan, for a really cheesy taste. Served with a whipped mustard butter they are just gorgeous. Some crispy pancetta sprinkled on top would be very tasty, too.

First make the mustard butter. Beat the butter with a wooden spoon until really light and creamy. Add both types of mustard and season with salt and black pepper. Mix to combine, then add the chopped chives. Lay a sheet of clingfilm/plastic wrap or baking parchment on the work surface and lay the butter on top in a rough sausage shape. Roll the butter into a neat log roughly 2 cm/¾ inch in diameter. Twist the ends to seal and chill the butter for about 2 hours until firm.

Preheat the oven to 200°C (400°F) Gas 6.

Sift the plain/all-purpose flour, spelt flour, baking powder, mustard powder and cayenne pepper into a large mixing bowl. Season well with black pepper and a pinch of salt. Add the chilled, diced butter and rub into the dry ingredients using your fingertips. When there are only very small specks of butter still visible add the grated Cheddar, Gruyère and Parmesan cheeses and mix to combine.

Make a well in the middle of the mixture and pour in the buttermilk and milk. Use a palette knife to mix into a dough, then very lightly bring the mixture together with your hands to a rough ball.

Turn the dough out onto a lightly floured surface and knead for 10 seconds. Flatten or roll out to a thickness of 1.5–2 cm/⅝–¾ inch. Use the cookie cutter to stamp out rounds and arrange on the prepared baking sheet, leaving a little space between each scone to allow for spreading during baking. Gather the dough scraps into a ball, re-roll and stamp out more scones. Brush the top of the scones with a little milk, scatter with the extra cheeses and a pinch of cayenne pepper.

Bake on the middle shelf of the preheated oven for about 13–15 minutes until well-risen and golden brown. Cool on a wire rack.

Split the scones in half and spread with the mustard butter to serve.

Inspired by the deli sandwiches of New York, this open sandwich (or tartine) is a tribute to an American classic. You could of course use salt beef or corned beef but I love pastrami and it goes really well with the nutty Emmental and sweet American-style mustard. The thousand-island coleslaw adds a really nice tang and crunch to the sandwich, too.

Pastrami and Emmental open sandwich *with thousand-island coleslaw on brown rye*

8 slices rye sourdough bread
100 g/6½ tablespoons butter, softened
4 teaspoons smooth American or Dijon mustard
8 Emmental cheese slices
12 slices pastrami
8 small gherkins
salt and freshly ground black pepper, to taste

COLESLAW
¼ white cabbage, finely shredded
2 large carrots, grated
1–2 tablespoons white wine vinegar
2 rounded tablespoons thousand-island dressing or mayonnaise

Serves 8

Start by making the coleslaw. Put the white cabbage in a large mixing bowl with the carrots. Add the white wine vinegar and thousand-island dressing or mayonnaise. Mix well, season with salt and black pepper. Cover and chill for at least 4 hours but preferably overnight.

The next day lay the bread slices out on the work surface and spread with butter. Season with salt and black pepper and thinly spread each slice with a little mustard. Top the bread with the cheese slices and cover with a mound of the coleslaw mixture – drained of any excess liquid.

Arrange the pastrami slices on top and garnish with thinly sliced gherkins. Spoon over a little extra mustard and serve the sandwich whole or cut in half.

Open sandwiches or tartines have been incredibly fashionable over the last few years and simply means 'toasts' in French. This tartine of red wine poached pear, crispy endive and creamy Stilton cheese really works well in the autumn, especially with the honey-roasted walnuts on top. Reduce the poaching liquor for a rich and sumptuous drizzle.

Red wine poached pear, Stilton and endive *on walnut bread*

2 pears
300 ml/1¼ cups red wine
50 g/¼ cup golden caster/raw cane sugar
1 rounded tablespoon clear honey
1 orange
1 cinnamon stick
1 star anise
1 tablespoon balsamic vinegar
8 slices walnut or seeded bread
100 g/6½ tablespoons butter, softened
2 heads Belgian endive
200 g/6½ oz. Stilton cheese
salt and freshly ground black pepper, to taste

CARAMELIZED WALNUTS
75 g/¾ cup walnuts
clear honey, to drizzle

Serves 8

Peel, quarter and core the pears and place in a pan with the red wine, sugar, honey, 2 strips of orange peel, removed from the fruit using a vegetable peeler, and the juice of half the orange. Pop in the cinnamon stick and star anise and set over a low heat to dissolve the sugar. Baste the pears and bring slowly to the boil, cover with a disc of baking parchment and continue to cook at a very gentle simmer until the fruit is tender – 15–30 minutes depending on the ripeness of the pears. Slide the pan off the heat and let the pears cool in the liquid. Leave the pears sitting in the poaching liquid for a good 2 hours or overnight after cooling.

Preheat the oven to 180°C (350°F) Gas 4.

Meanwhile, prepare the caramelized walnuts. Scatter the walnuts on a baking sheet and drizzle with honey. Toast in the preheated oven for 5–10 minutes, turning once.

Lift the pears from the pan using a slotted spoon and set aside. Add the balsamic vinegar to the poaching liquid and return the pan to the heat. Bring to the boil, reduce to a simmer and continue to cook until the poaching liquid is thick and syrupy and has reduced to just 2–3 tablespoons.

Spread the bread slices with butter and season with salt and black pepper.

Trim the endive, remove the outer leaves and separate each head into individual leaves. Arrange the leaves on top of the buttered bread, slice the poached pears and arrange on top. Crumble the Stilton and scatter on top of the pears. Finally, finish with a sprinkle of caramelized walnuts and a drizzle of the reduced poaching syrup.

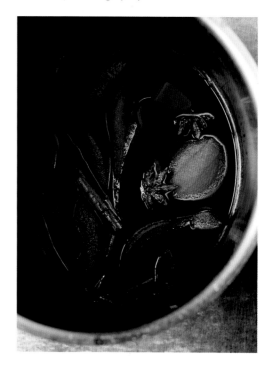

Eccles cakes originate from the English town of Eccles and are traditionally served with Lancashire cheese or occasionally Stilton. I've added a Spanish twist to my Eccles cakes mixture by soaking the currants in rich and dark Pedro Ximénez – the king of sweet sherries. Instead of Lancashire cheese, I'm serving mine with Manchego because it pairs beautifully with the flavour notes of the sherry.

Eccles cakes *with Pedro Ximénez and Manchego cheese*

500 g/1 lb. all-butter puff pastry/dough, thawed if frozen
1 egg white, lightly beaten
1–2 tablespoons golden caster/raw cane sugar
Manchego cheese, to serve

FILLING
150 g/1 cup dried Zante currants
2–3 tablespoons Pedro Ximénez (PX) sherry
30 g/2½ tablespoons demerara/turbinado sugar
½ teaspoon ground allspice
freshly grated nutmeg
zest of ½ orange
25 g/2 tablespoons butter, melted

a 6.5-cm/2½-inch, 7-cm/2¾-inch and 8-cm/3¼-inch round cookie cutter
2 baking sheets lined with baking parchment

Makes about 24

Prepare the filling first. Combine the currants with the Pedro Ximénez, demerara/turbinado sugar, spices and orange zest in a small pan. Set over a low heat to warm the sherry but do not allow it to boil. Remove the pan from the heat, add the butter, stir well and set aside for about 2 hours to allow the currants to absorb the warm liquid and become plump and juicy.

Roll out half of the puff pastry/dough on a lightly floured work surface to a thickness of no more than 2 mm/$\frac{1}{16}$ inch. Using the smallest and largest cookie cutters stamp out as many discs as you can – you will need an equal number of small and large discs as one is the base and the other one the top for each cake. Repeat with the remaining pastry/dough.

Arrange the smaller discs on the prepared baking sheets leaving a little space between each one. Drain the currants of any excess liquid and spoon a rounded teaspoon of the plump currants into the middle of each disc.

Brush around the edges with a little water and top with the larger pastry discs, pressing the edges to seal. Chill the Eccles cakes in the fridge for 20 minutes.

Preheat the oven to 190°C (375°F) Gas 5.

Press the medium-sized cookie cutter over each Eccles cake to neaten and trim the edges and cut 3 short lines in the top of each one.

Brush the beaten egg white over the top of each cake, sprinkle with golden caster/raw cane sugar and bake on the middle shelf of the preheated oven for about 20 minutes until the pastry/dough is well-risen, crisp and golden brown.

Leave to cool slightly before serving with Manchego cheese.

These triple chocolate cookies are for all the chocoholics out there… not only does the cookie dough have cocoa powder and white chocolate chunks in it, it also has melted chocolate to add a real depth of flavour. Once they are baked and cooled, drizzle with some melted milk/semi-sweet chocolate for an extra chocolatey hit.

Triple chocolate cookies

225 g/8 oz. dark/
   bittersweet chocolate
   (55–65 %), chopped
125 g/1 stick butter,
   softened
200 g/1 cup soft light
   brown sugar
2 eggs, lightly beaten
1 teaspoon vanilla extract
185 g/1½ cups plain/
   all-purpose flour
40 g/⅓ cup cocoa
   powder
1 teaspoon bicarbonate
   of soda/baking soda
a pinch of salt
150 g/5 oz. white
   chocolate, chopped
100 g/3½ oz. white,
   milk/semi-sweet or
   dark/bittersweet
   chocolate, chopped,
   to decorate

*2 baking sheets lined
with baking parchment*

Makes 30–35

Melt the dark/bittersweet chocolate in a heatproof bowl suspended over a pan of barely simmering water. Stir until smooth and leave to cool slightly.

Cream the butter with the soft light brown sugar in a stand mixer until pale and light. Scrape down the sides of the bowl with a rubber spatula and gradually add the beaten eggs, mixing well between each addition. Add the vanilla extract and mix again to combine.

Add the melted dark/bittersweet chocolate and mix until combined.

Sift in the flour, cocoa powder, bicarbonate of soda/baking soda and add the salt. Mix again until nearly smooth. Add the chopped white chocolate and fold in until the chunks are well distributed throughout the dough.

Lay a sheet of baking parchment on the work surface and spoon half of the dough on top in a neat sausage shape. Roll the dough using the baking parchment into a neat, tight 4–5-cm/1½–2-inch diameter

log and wrap up tightly. Repeat with another sheet of parchment and the remaining dough. Chill the logs in the fridge for 2 hours or in the freezer for 45 minutes until firm.

Preheat the oven to 170°C (325°F) Gas 3.

Unwrap the dough and, using a sharp knife, slice into neat rounds each about 1 cm/ ⅜ inch thick and arrange on the baking sheets, leaving a little space between each cookie to allow for spreading during cooking.

Bake on the middle shelf of the preheated oven for 10–12 minutes until just firm. Leave to cool on the baking sheet for 5 minutes, then transfer to a wire rack to cool completely.

Melt the remaining white, milk/semi-sweet or dark/bittersweet chocolate as above and, using a teaspoon, drizzle over the cookies in swirls. Leave until set before serving.

PBJ cookie sandwiches

325 g/2½ cups plain/
all-purpose flour
½ rounded teaspoon
bicarbonate of
soda/baking soda
a pinch of salt
175 g/1½ sticks butter,
softened
50 g/3½ tablespoons
crunchy peanut butter
100 g/½ cup caster/
granulated sugar
175 g/¾ cup plus
2 tablespoons light
muscovado sugar
2 teaspoons vanilla extract
2 eggs, lightly beaten
150 g/1¼ cups
dark/bittersweet
chocolate chips
150 g/1¼ cup salted
peanuts, roughly
chopped
3–4 tablespoons good-
quality raspberry
jam/jelly, to serve

PEANUT BUTTER FROSTING
250 g/8 oz. cream cheese
175 g/1²/₃ cups smooth
peanut butter
25 g/2 tablespoons butter,
softened
50 g/¹/₃ cup icing/
confectioners' sugar
25 g/2 tablespoons soft
light brown sugar
1 teaspoon vanilla extract
1 tablespoon whole milk

*2 large baking sheets covered
with baking parchment
a disposable piping/
pastry bag*

Makes about 20

These are pretty special! I love peanut butter and jam/jelly, and they work so well as a double filling in these cookie sandwiches. Be careful though, you may not be able to stop at just one!

Sift together the flour and bicarbonate of soda/baking soda in a large mixing bowl, add the salt and set aside.

In a stand mixer, cream together the butter, peanut butter, caster/granulated and light muscovado sugar until very soft and light – this will take 3–5 minutes. Use a rubber spatula to scrape down the sides of the bowl, add the vanilla extract and mix again. Gradually add the beaten eggs and mix until incorporated. Add the sifted dry ingredients and mix again until barely combined. Add the chocolate chips and peanuts, and fold in using a metal spoon or large rubber spatula.

Lay a sheet of baking parchment on the work surface and spoon half of the dough on top in a neat sausage shape. Roll the dough using the baking parchment into a neat, tight 5-cm/2-inch diameter log and wrap up tightly. Repeat with another sheet of parchment and the remaining dough. Chill the logs in the fridge for at least 4 hours or ideally overnight until firm.

Preheat the oven to 170°C (325°F) Gas 3.

Unwrap the dough logs and, using a sharp knife, slice into neat rounds each about 2 mm/¹/₁₆ inch thick and arrange on the baking sheets, leaving a little space between each cookie to allow for them to spread during cooking.

Bake on the middle shelf of the preheated oven for 10–12 minutes until the edges of the cookies are golden brown and the middle is still slightly soft.

Leave to cool on the baking sheet for 3–4 minutes, then transfer to a wire rack and leave until completely cold.

To make the peanut butter frosting, scoop the cream cheese, peanut butter and butter into a bowl and beat until smooth. Sift in the icing/confectioners' sugar, add the soft light brown sugar, vanilla extract and milk, and beat again until smooth and creamy. Scoop into the piping/pastry bag and set aside.

Turn half of the cookies upside down on the work surface so that they are flat side uppermost. Pipe a ring of frosting onto the surface of each cookie and fill the space in the middle with ½ teaspoon of raspberry jam/jelly. Sandwich with the naked cookies and serve.

I remember as a child, every Sunday morning, we'd get home from church, and Mum and Dad would have a coffee (with a dash of brandy in it!) and an egg custard tart. I never used to like them then but have grown to adore them! Adding malted milk powder to the pastry and malt extract to the custard filling gives the tarts a lovely flavour and the little hint of orange in the custard filling lifts it to a whole new level.

Malty egg custard tarts

175 g/1⅓ cups plain/
  all-purpose flour
25 g/2 tablespoons
  malted milk powder
a pinch of salt
100 g/6½ tablespoons
  butter, chilled and
  diced
30 g/2½ tablespoons
  icing/confectioners'
  sugar
1 egg, lightly beaten
freshly grated nutmeg,
  to decorate

CUSTARD FILLING
4 large egg yolks
50 g/¼ cup caster/
  granulated sugar
1 tablespoon malt extract
1 teaspoon orange zest
a pinch of salt
225 ml/scant 1 cup
  double/heavy cream
50 ml/3½ tablespoons
  whole milk

*12 x 8-cm/3¼-inch mini
tart pans or a 12-hole
muffin pan, greased
a 9–10-cm/3½–4-inch
fluted cookie cutter
baking beans (optional)*

Makes 12

Tip the flour and malted milk powder into the bowl of a food processor, add the salt and the butter. Pulse the butter into the flour until it is pale and sand-like in texture. Add the icing/confectioners' sugar and mix to combine. Add the beaten egg and pulse again until the dough starts to come together.

Tip the dough out onto the work surface and use your hands to bring it together into a neat ball. Flatten into a disc, cover in clingfilm/plastic wrap and chill for at least 1 hour until firm.

Roll out the chilled dough on a lightly floured work surface to a thickness of no more than 2 mm/¹⁄₁₆ inch. Using the cookie cutter, stamp out 12 discs from the dough. Gently press the pastry discs into the prepared tart pans, trying not to stretch the dough but making sure that the pans are evenly lined.

Arrange on a baking sheet and chill in the fridge for 20 minutes.

Preheat the oven to 170°C (325°F) Gas 3.

Line the tart cases with a square of baking parchment or foil and fill with baking beans or rice. Bake in the preheated oven for 10 minutes until pale golden and starting to crisp. Remove the tarts from the oven and reduce the heat to 150°C (300°F) Gas 2. Remove the baking beans or rice and parchment or foil, and set aside.

Next, make the custard filling. In a medium mixing bowl, whisk the eggs yolks with the caster/granulated sugar, malt extract and salt until smooth. Add the orange zest and mix again to combine. Pour the double/heavy cream and milk into the bowl and mix again until smooth and thoroughly combined.

Pour the custard into a jug/pitcher and divide between the tart cases. Grate a little nutmeg over each tart and carefully slide the baking sheet back into the oven on the middle shelf and bake in the cooler oven for 20–25 minutes until the custard has just set. Remove from the oven and leave to cool before carefully removing from the tart pans. Cool to room temperature before serving.

Two much-loved American desserts are pumpkin pie and pecan pie and I think they go really well together. This recipe calls for a spiced pastry with a pumpkin and maple syrup filling baked together with cinnamon and pecans.

Pumpkin and pecan pies

200 g/1²/₃ cups plain/ all-purpose flour

½ teaspoon ground cinnamon

100 g/6½ tablespoons butter, chilled and diced

a pinch of salt

30 g/2½ tablespoons icing/confectioners' sugar

1 egg, lightly beaten

32 pecan halves, to decorate

3 tablespoons apricot jam/jelly (page 11), to glaze

FILLING

100 g/²/₃ cup pecans

2 eggs

150 g/²/₃ cup pumpkin purée

1 teaspoon ground cinnamon

75 g/¼ cup maple syrup

3 tablespoons double/ heavy cream

12 x 7-cm/3-inch mini tart pans or a 12-hole muffin pan
9–10-cm/3¼–4-inch cookie cutter
baking beans (optional)

Makes 12

Tip the flour into the bowl of a food processor, add the ground cinnamon, salt and the chilled, diced butter. Pulse until pale and sand-like in texture. Add the icing/ confectioners' sugar and mix to combine. Add the beaten egg and pulse again until the dough starts to come together.

Tip the dough out onto the work surface and use your hands to bring it together into a neat ball. Flatten into a disc, cover in clingfilm/plastic wrap and chill in the fridge for at least 1 hour until firm.

Roll out the chilled dough on a lightly floured work surface to a thickness of no more than 2 mm/¹/₁₆ inch. Using the cookie cutter, stamp out 12 discs. Gently press the pastry discs into the prepared tart pans, trying not to stretch the dough until evenly lined. Prick the bases with a fork and arrange on a baking sheet and chill in the fridge for 20 minutes.

Preheat the oven to 170°C (325°F) Gas 3.

Line the tart cases with a square of baking parchment or foil and fill with baking beans or rice. Bake in the preheated oven for 10 minutes until pale golden and starting to crisp. Remove the baking beans or rice and parchment or foil, and bake for another 1–2 minutes to dry out the bases.

Meanwhile, toast the pecans for the filling. Tip onto a baking sheet and toast for 4 minutes on the shelf below the tart cases.

Remove from the oven, roughly chop and when cooled slightly, divide between the tarts.

To make the filling, break the eggs into a mixing bowl, add the remaining ingredients, and whisk to combine. Scoop the mixture into a jug/pitcher and pour into the tarts, filling them evenly. Top each filled tart with the pecan halves and bake on the middle shelf of the oven for a further 12–15 minutes until just set. Remove from the oven and leave to cool to room temperature.

Warm the apricot jam/jelly in a small pan until runny, strain into a bowl through a fine mesh sieve/strainer and brush neatly over the top of each tart. Leave to set before serving.

Spiced pumpkin and apple cakes

150 g/1 stick plus 2
   tablespoons butter,
   softened
100 g/½ cup caster/
   granulated sugar
50 g/¼ cup soft light
   brown sugar
2 eggs, lightly beaten
150 g/1 cup plus 2
   tablespoons plain/
   all-purpose flour
1 teaspoon ground
   cinnamon
1 teaspoon baking powder
½ teaspoon bicarbonate
   of soda/baking soda
a pinch of salt
2 small apples, peeled,
   cored and grated
150 g/10 tablespoons
   pumpkin purée

PUMPKIN SEED PRALINE
75 g/5 tablespoons
   caster/granulated
   sugar
75 g/½ cup pumpkin
   seeds
a pinch of salt

CINNAMON ICING
175 g/1¼ cups icing/
   confectioners' sugar
1 teaspoon ground
   cinnamon
2 tablespoons lemon
   juice or water

*a 12-hole mini bundt/
kugelhopf pan (7 cm/
3 inches at the widest
point), well greased
with melted butter
a disposable piping/
pastry bag*

Makes 12

These little bundt cakes are simply delicious. The rich spiced pumpkin cake with apple is light and fluffy, topped with a cinnamon icing and finished with a pumpkin seed praline. Add a pinch of salt to the praline for a lovely finish.

Preheat the oven to 180°C (350°F) Gas 4.

Cream the softened butter with the caster/granulated and soft light brown sugars until pale and light – this is easiest and quickest in a stand mixer. Scrape down the sides of the bowl with a rubber spatula, then gradually add the beaten eggs, mixing well between each addition.

Sift in the flour, cinnamon, baking powder and bicarbonate of soda/baking soda and add the salt. Mix to just combine. Add the apples and pumpkin purée, and mix again until smooth.

Spoon the mixture into the cake pan, filling them to within 2–3 mm/⅛ inch from the top to allow space for them to rise during cooking. Spread level with the back of a teaspoon and bake on the middle shelf of the preheated oven for 20–25 minutes until golden brown, well-risen and a skewer inserted into the middle of the cakes comes out clean.

Leave the cakes to cool in the pan for 2 minutes, then carefully turn out onto a wire rack to cool completely.

To make the pumpkin praline, tip the caster/granulated sugar into a small pan and add 1 tablespoon of water. Set the pan over a low heat to dissolve the sugar, increase the heat and bring to the boil without stirring. Continue to cook until the syrup becomes an amber-coloured caramel. Add the pumpkin seeds, stir well to coat and continue to cook for another 20 seconds. Tip the caramel out of the pan onto a sheet of baking parchment, spread it out thinly using a palette knife and set aside to cool and set firm.

To make the cinnamon icing, sift the icing/confectioners' sugar into a bowl and add the ground cinnamon and whisking constantly add enough lemon juice and/or water to make a smooth drizzly icing that will just coat the back of a spoon. Pour the icing into the piping/pastry bag and drizzle over the top and sides of each cake.

Break the pumpkin seed praline into pieces and put in a sandwich bag. Bash with the end of a rolling pin, then scatter the praline dust over the top of the cakes before serving.

Although the origin of this marzipan-wrapped chequerboard cake is unclear, it's thought that the cake was named in honour of the marriage of Queen Victoria's granddaughter to Prince Louis of Battenberg in 1884.

Vanilla and chocolate Battenberg

200 g/1¾ sticks butter, softened
200 g/1 cup caster/ granulated sugar
4 eggs, beaten
2 teaspoons vanilla extract
150 g/1 cup plus 2 tablespoons plain/ all-purpose flour
50 g/½ cup ground hazelnuts or almonds
2 teaspoons baking powder
a generous pinch of salt
3 tablespoons whole milk

CHOCOLATE CAKE
50 g/1½ oz. dark/ bittersweet chocolate, melted
1 tablespoon cocoa powder

TO FINISH
4 tablespoons chocolate and hazelnut spread (page 15) or Nutella
2–3 tablespoons apricot jam/jelly (page 11)
400 g/14 oz. marzipan
1 teaspoon cocoa powder
icing/confectioners' sugar, for dusting

2 x 20-cm/8-inch square cake pans, greased and lined with buttered baking parchment

Makes 20 slices

Preheat the oven to 180°C (350°F) Gas 4.

To make the cake batter, cream the butter and caster/granulated sugar until pale, light and fluffy – this will take about 3 minutes in a stand mixer and longer by hand. Gradually add the beaten eggs, mixing well between each addition and scraping down the sides of the bowl with a rubber spatula from time to time. Add the vanilla extract and mix again. Sift in the flour, ground nuts, baking powder and salt, add the milk and mix again until smooth.

Scoop half of the batter into one of the prepared cake pans and spread level using a palette knife. Set the remaining batter aside.

Bake the cake on the middle shelf of the preheated oven for about 15 minutes until golden and a wooden skewer inserted into the middle of the cake comes out clean.

Rest in the pan for 3–4 minutes, then turn out onto a wire rack to cool.

Meanwhile, prepare the chocolate cake. Add the melted chocolate to the reserved cake batter. Mix until smooth, spoon into the second cake pan and bake and cool as above. Cover both cakes with clingfilm/plastic wrap and leave overnight. You can build the Battenberg now if you wish, but resting overnight makes slicing the cakes easier.

To build the Battenberg, lay the cakes on the work surface and, using a serrated knife, trim the rounded tops off the cakes to make them level. Spread the top of the vanilla cake with chocolate and hazelnut spread, then lay the chocolate cake on top, gently pressing them together. Trim away the sides of the cake and, with the help of a ruler, cut into 4 even strips. Cut each of these strips in half again so that you have 8 strips each measuring roughly 18 x 2 cm/7 x ¾ inch. Flip one cake strip over onto its side and spread with an even layer of chocolate and hazelnut spread. Take a second strip, rotate it 180° and lay it on top of the first strip to form a chequerboard cake. Set aside and repeat with the remaining strips.

Warm the apricot jam/jelly in a small pan set over a low heat. Remove from the heat before boiling and strain through a fine mesh sieve/ strainer into a bowl. Set aside.

Cut the marzipan into quarters. Lightly dust the work surface with icing/confectioners' sugar and roll out one piece of marzipan to an 18-cm/7-inch square. Brush with warmed apricot jam/jelly. Lay one of the cakes on top of the marzipan against the edge nearest to you, trim the edge of the marzipan to size, then roll the cake over in the marzipan so that all four sides are covered evenly. Trim off any excess marzipan and repeat with the second cake. Set aside.

Add the cocoa powder to the other two pieces of marzipan and knead to combine smoothly. Divide the chocolate marzipan in half, roll and cover the last two cakes as above.

Cut the Battenbergs into slices to serve.

Similar to Australia's Lamington cakes, these are often described as English madeleines and can be cooked in tall dariole moulds. I like to dip my squares of cake in warmed raspberry jam/jelly because it works so well with the coconut. You could even dip them in passionfruit curd (page 12), then the coconut for a tropical twist.

Jam and coconut cakes

175 g/1½ sticks butter, softened

175 g/¾ cup plus 2 tablespoons caster/granulated sugar

3 large eggs, lightly beaten

1 teaspoon vanilla bean paste

150 g/1 cup plus 2 tablespoons plain/all-purpose flour

30 g/2½ tablespoons cornflour/cornstarch

1½ teaspoons baking powder

a pinch of salt

2 tablespoons whole milk

TO DECORATE

450 g/1½ cups good-quality raspberry jam/jelly

350 g/4⅔ cups desiccated/shredded coconut

a 20-cm/8-inch square cake pan, greased and base-lined with buttered baking parchment

Makes 25

Preheat the oven to 180°C (375°F) Gas 4.

Cream together the butter and caster/granulated sugar until really pale and fluffy – this will take about 5 minutes. Gradually add the beaten eggs, mixing well between each addition and adding a little of the plain/all-purpose flour if the mixture looks curdled at any stage. Sift in the plain/all-purpose flour, cornflour/cornstarch and baking powder and add the salt and milk. Mix again until smooth.

Spoon the batter into the prepared cake pan and bake on the middle shelf of the preheated oven for 25–30 minutes until well risen, pale golden and a skewer inserted in the middle of the cake comes out clean.

Cool in the pan for 5 minutes, then turn out onto a wire rack to cool completely. Cover with clingfilm/plastic wrap and leave overnight to make cutting easier.

Using a long serrated knife, trim the sides of the cake to neaten, then cut into 25 even 4-cm/1½-inch squares.

Spoon the jam/jelly into a small pan, add 2 tablespoons of water and melt over a low heat until the jam/jelly is smooth and runny. Tip the desiccated/shredded coconut onto a large baking sheet.

Taking one square cake at a time, spear it onto a large fork and dip into the hot jam/jelly to completely coat. Allow any excess jam/jelly to drip back into the pan, then roll the cake in the desiccated/shredded coconut to cover in an even layer. Arrange on a clean sheet of baking parchment and repeat with the remaining cakes. Leave to set for 1 hour at room temperature before serving.

Black Forest fondant fancies

150 g/1 stick plus 2 tablespoons butter, softened

100 g/½ cup caster/granulated sugar

100 g/½ cup soft light brown sugar

3 eggs, lightly beaten

1 teaspoon vanilla extract

200 g/1⅔ cups plain/all-purpose flour

½ teaspoon bicarbonate of soda/baking soda

1 teaspoon baking powder

a pinch of salt

40 g/⅓ cup cocoa powder

3 tablespoons whole milk

5 tablespoons cherry jam/jelly (page 11)

100 g/3½ oz. marzipan

50 g/1½ oz. white chocolate, melted, to decorate

VANILLA AND KIRSCH BUTTERCREAM

125 g/1 stick butter, softened

150 g/1 cup icing/confectioners' sugar

1 tablespoon Kirsch

1 teaspoon vanilla bean paste

CHOCOLATE FONDANT

500 g/3½ cups fondant icing/confectioners' sugar

3 tablespoons cocoa powder

a 20-cm/8-inch square cake pan, greased and lined with buttered baking parchment

1–2 disposable piping/pastry bags

Makes 16

Along with scones and finger sandwiches, for me fondant fancies are an absolute must for afternoon tea. They evoke memories of childhood and these have a 'Black Forest' twist with the addition of chocolate, cherries and Kirsch.

Preheat the oven to 180°C (350°F) Gas 4.

Cream the butter with the caster/granulated and soft light brown sugars in a stand mixer for 3–4 minutes until pale and light. Scrape down the bowl with a rubber spatula and gradually add the beaten eggs, mixing well between each addition. Add the vanilla extract and mix again until combined.

Sift in the flour, bicarbonate of soda/baking soda and baking powder, and add the salt. Mix the cocoa powder with 3–4 tablespoons of boiling water, then add to the mixture with the milk, and beat until smooth. Spoon the mixture into the prepared cake pan and spread level with the back of a spoon.

Bake on the middle shelf of the preheated oven for 30–35 minutes or until a skewer inserted into the middle of the cake comes out clean. Cool in the pan, then turn out of the pan, peel off the baking parchment, turn the cake the right way up and leave to cool completely on a wire rack.

To prepare the vanilla and Kirsch buttercream, beat the butter until very soft, pale and light. Gradually add the icing/confectioners' sugar, mixing well between each addition and when it has all been incorporated add the Kirsch and the vanilla bean paste. Mix again.

Using a serrated knife, slice the rounded top off the cake to give it a totally flat and smooth top, then cut the cake in half horizontally. Carefully lift the top half of the cake off and set aside. Using a palette knife, spread half of the buttercream in a smooth layer on the bottom cake layer. Top the buttercream with half of the cherry jam/jelly and replace the top cake layer. Gently press together, then spread the remaining cherry jam/jelly on top.

Lightly dust the work surface with icing/confectioners' sugar and roll out the marzipan to a 20-cm/8-inch square. Carefully lift over the cake covering the jam/jelly. Using the serrated knife trim the edges of the cake, then cut into 16 squares.

Spoon the remaining buttercream into one of the piping/pastry bags and pipe a small mound of buttercream on top of each square.

To make the chocolate fondant, sift the fondant icing/confectioners' sugar and cocoa powder into a mixing bowl, and whisking constantly, add enough water to make an icing that coats the back of a spoon.

Taking one square cake at a time, spear it onto a large fork and spoon the fondant over the top and sides of the cake allowing any excess to drip back into the bowl. Gently tap the fork on the sides of the bowl to allow any excess icing to run down the sides, then carefully slide the cake off the fork onto a wire rack set over a sheet of baking parchment. Repeat with the remaining cakes, then leave them to dry for 1 hour.

Drizzle the melted white chocolate over the cakes and leave to set before serving.

On my recent honeymoon in New York, my wife and I ate at the famous Gramercy Tavern and it blew us away! It's one of America's most beloved restaurants, serving food for almost 20 years. Pastry Chef Miroslav Uskokovic's mother used to make this cake all the time during sour cherry season and the cake is very common in northern Serbia and Hungary. The first time Miro made the cake in America was while working as a sous chef at the Jean-Georges restaurant. Jean-Georges himself found this cake irresistible and would stop by the pastry kitchen almost every day for a slice. When Miro became the pastry chef at Gramercy Tavern he put his cake on the menu and paired it with some other traditional Serbian flavours like poppy seeds, farmers' cheese and chervil, and the dessert was a great success.

Mom's sour cherry cake

320 g/2½ cups plain/all-purpose flour
10 g/2½ teaspoons baking powder
a pinch of salt
250 g/1¼ cups caster/granulated sugar
2 eggs
15 g/1 tablespoon vanilla extract
225 ml/scant 1 cup sunflower oil, or other neutral vegetable oil
225 ml/scant 1 cup whole milk

500 g/2½ cups fresh or frozen pitted sour cherries (if frozen, do not defrost)
a handful of flaked/slivered almonds
icing/confectioners' sugar, for dusting

a 27-cm/10½-inch square baking pan, lined with baking parchment

Serves 16

Preheat the oven to 160°C (325°F) Gas 3.

Sift together the flour and baking powder in a large mixing bowl. Set aside.

Combine the salt, sugar and eggs in a separate bowl and beat with a handheld electric mixer until the mixture triples in volume and leaves a trail when you drag a spoon through it. Add the vanilla extract and stir through.

In a slow stream pour in the oil, mixing well, followed by the milk.

Add the sifted flour mixture and mix just enough to combine.

Spread evenly in the prepared pan and sprinkle all over with sour cherries. Sprinkle with flaked/slivered almonds for extra flavour and texture.

Bake in the preheated oven for 25–30 minutes or until a skewer inserted in the middle of the cake comes out clean.

Cool, then cut into squares and sprinkle with icing/confectioners' sugar before serving.

Coffee, walnut and cardamom cake

4–6 cardamom pods
4 teaspoons instant
coffee granules
225 g/1 stick plus 6
tablespoons butter,
softened
125 g/scant ⅔ cup
golden caster/raw cane
sugar
100 g/½ cup light
muscovado sugar
4 eggs, lightly beaten
225 g/1¾ cups plain/
all-purpose flour
1 tablespoon cocoa
powder
2 teaspoons baking
powder
1 teaspoon bicarbonate
of soda/baking soda
a pinch of salt
2 tablespoons whole
milk, at room
temperature
100 g/1 cup walnuts,
chopped and toasted
1¼ quantity Meringue
buttercream (page 54)

WALNUT PRALINE
100 g/½ cup golden
caster/raw cane sugar
100 g/1 cup walnuts

*3 x 20-cm/8-inch cake
pans, greased and base-
lined with buttered baking
parchment
a sugar thermometer*

Serves 8

Another much-loved cake in the UK is coffee and walnut cake, and I've given it a little twist by adding cardamom to the cake batter. I've also added the coffee to the light and fluffy Italian meringue buttercream, which brings with it an autumnal warmth. The walnut praline used to decorate the cake adds a really lovely texture.

Preheat the oven to 180°C (350°F) Gas 4.

Start by making the cake batter. Crush the cardamom pods using a pestle and mortar and pick out the husk leaving the little black seeds in the mortar. Grind the seeds to a fine powder. In a small bowl dissolve the coffee granules in 3 teaspoons of boiling water.

Tip the butter into the bowl of a stand mixer, add the golden caster/raw cane and light muscovado sugars, and cream until pale and light – this will take at least 3–4 minutes. Gradually add the beaten eggs, mixing well between each addition and scraping down the sides of the bowl with a rubber spatula from time to time. Add the crushed cardamom seeds and coffee and mix again to combine. Sift in the flour, cocoa powder, baking powder and bicarbonate of soda/baking soda and add the salt. Add the milk and mix again until thoroughly combined and the batter is smooth. Add the chopped toasted walnuts and fold in.

Weigh the cake mix and divide it evenly between the 3 prepared cake pans. Bake on the middle shelf of the preheated oven for about 20 minutes until well risen and a skewer inserted into the middle of the cakes comes out clean. Leave the cakes to rest in the pans for 3 minutes, then carefully turn out onto a wire rack to cool completely.

Next, prepare the walnut praline. While the oven is still on, toast the walnuts on a baking sheet for 3–4 minutes. Roughly chop and set aside. Tip the golden caster/raw cane sugar into a small pan, add 1–2 tablespoons of water and set over a low heat without stirring to dissolve the sugar. Bring to the boil and continue to cook until the syrup becomes an amber-coloured caramel, swirling the pan so that the caramel cooks evenly. Tip the nuts into the pan, stir to coat and cook for another 30 seconds. Quickly tip the nutty caramel out onto a sheet of baking parchment and leave until hardened and cold.

Break the caramel into chunks and whizz in the food processor until finely chopped. Store in an airtight container until needed – sugar loses its crunch if left exposed.

To build the cake, place one layer on a serving plate and spread with 3 tablespoons of the meringue buttercream. Top this with a second cake layer and spread with more meringue buttercream. Add the third cake layer and using a palette knife spread the remaining meringue buttercream over the top and sides of the cake. Press the walnut praline around the base and top of the cake and serve.

Olive and anchovy whirls

Fig and ricotta crispbreads *with pistachios,
mint and pomegranate molasses*

Gougères

Nans' Welsh cakes

Chocolate and cherry scones *with
Kirsch and vanilla Chantilly cream*

Veronica's gingerbreads

Golden ginger custard creams

Treacle tarts *with ginger cake and orange*

Harrods Mince pie brownies

Hazelnut, apricot and vanilla roulade

Strawberry and sherry trifles

Spiced chocolate domes *with
brandy-soaked raisins and cacao nibs*

Winter celebration

These cute little pinwheels take their inspiration from two popular savoury canapés; palmiers and anchovy straws. Some of the best puff pastry-based canapés I've had were at The Waterside Inn at Bray where they also serve olive straws. The olives and anchovies work really well together to make a tasty tapenade and go superbly with some crisp chilled fizz.

Olive and anchovy whirls

70 g/¾ cup pitted/stoned black olives (I use Crespo pitted dry black olives in herbs)

30 g/1 oz. anchovy fillets in olive oil, chopped

1 garlic clove, crushed

1 tablespoon finely chopped fresh parsley

freshly ground black pepper, to taste

1–2 tablespoons olive oil

500 g/1 lb. all-butter puff pastry/dough, thawed if frozen

2 baking sheets lined with baking parchment

Makes about 40

Tip the olives, anchovies, crushed garlic, chopped parsley and a good grinding of black pepper into the bowl of a food processor. Add a little of the olive oil and blend until finely chopped and almost the consistency of a paste – you may not need all of the olive oil.

Cut the pastry in half – you will find it easier to work with two smaller pieces rather than one large piece. Roll out one piece on a lightly floured work surface into a rectangle measuring 40 x 20 cm/16 x 8 inches. Using a palette knife spread half of the olive paste in a smooth layer over the pastry and trim the edges of the pastry. Starting at one of the shorter (20-cm/8-inch) ends roll the pastry into a tight spiral with the paste inside.

Wrap in clingfilm/plastic wrap and repeat with the second piece of pastry and remaining olive paste.

Put the rolls in the freezer for about 2 hours until firm.

Preheat the oven to 190°C (375°F) Gas 5.

Slice each pastry log into discs about 5 mm/ ¼ inch thick and arrange on the prepared baking sheets leaving a little space between each one. Bake on the middle shelf of the preheated oven for about 20 minutes or until crisp and golden brown.

Serve warm from the oven.

These roasted fig and ricotta crispbreads make delightful canapés for a New Year's Eve party as well as one of your savouries for afternoon tea. What makes them super-special is the drizzle of pomegranate molasses and mixed chopped parsley and mint – it's a taste explosion!

Fig and ricotta crispbreads *with pistachios, mint and pomegranate molasses*

6 ripe figs
2 tablespoons extra
    virgin olive oil
3 tablespoons
    pomegranate
    molasses
250 g/8 oz. ricotta cheese
24 round Scandinavian-
    style crispbreads
50 g/½ cup shelled
    unsalted pistachios,
    roughly chopped
2 tablespoons roughly
    chopped fresh flat-leaf
    parsley
2 tablespoons roughly
    chopped fresh mint
salt and freshly ground
    black pepper, to taste

a baking sheet lined with foil

Makes 24

Preheat the grill/broiler to high.

Cut the figs in half through the stalks and arrange cut-side uppermost on the prepared baking sheet. Drizzle with a little oil and 1 tablespoon of the pomegranate molasses.

Place the dressed figs under the grill/broiler until juicy and bubbling. Remove from the heat and leave to cool.

Mix the ricotta with another tablespoon of the pomegranate molasses and season with salt and black pepper.

Lay the crispbreads on the work surface or on a serving tray and divide the ricotta between them, spreading it almost to the edges.

Cut each fig half in half again so that you have bite-sized quarters and arrange on top of the ricotta-spread crispbreads.

Scatter with pistachios, sprinkle with roughly chopped herbs and serve immediately.

Said to have originated in the French region of Burgundy, gougères are a simple, savoury choux/cream puff bun flavoured with cheese. Always served warm as an appetizer they can also be filled with cheese sauces or even ham or mushrooms. Here, I've kept them simple, flavoured with Parmesan and Gruyère, a little bit of fresh thyme and some spices.

Gougères

75 ml/5 tablespoons
   whole milk
60 g/½ stick butter
100 g/¾ cup plain/
   all-purpose flour
½ teaspoon cayenne
   pepper
½ teaspoon dry mustard
   powder
1 teaspoon chopped
   fresh thyme leaves
3 eggs, lightly beaten
60 g/¾ cup finely grated
   Parmesan cheese
60 g/½ cup grated
   Gruyère cheese
salt and freshly ground
   black pepper, to taste

*2–3 baking sheets lined
with baking parchment*

Makes about 40

Preheat the oven to 180°C (350°F) Gas 4.

Put 75 ml/5 tablespoons of water with the milk and butter into a medium pan and set over a medium heat. Stir constantly to melt the butter. As soon as the mixture comes to a rolling boil, reduce the heat slightly and working quickly and keeping the pan over a low heat, stir in the flour, cayenne pepper and mustard powder, and season well with salt and black pepper. Add the fresh thyme and beat vigorously until the mixture is smooth and cleanly leaves the sides of the pan – this will take about 2 minutes.

Transfer the dough to a stand mixer or mixing bowl (using an electric whisk) and leave to cool for 5 minutes. Then gradually beat in the beaten eggs 1 tablespoon at a time. You might not need all of the egg – when the dough is soft and smooth and drops off a spoon leaving a 'V' shape behind it is ready.

Add all but 1 rounded tablespoon of the grated cheeses and mix to combine.

Using dessertspoons, drop small mounds of dough onto each prepared baking sheet leaving plenty of space between each one – they should be no bigger than the size of a walnut. Scatter with the extra cheese and bake on the middle shelves of the preheated oven for 10–15 minutes until well-risen and golden brown. Remove from the oven and cool for 5 minutes before serving.

I owe a lot of my food memories to my Nans and her Welsh cakes are legendary in our family. Made in batches, she would wrap them in baking parchment and foil, and keep them in the freezer. We would return home after a visit with batches to go in our own freezers ready to enjoy when family friends came calling.

Nans' Welsh cakes

220 g/1¾ cups plain/
all-purpose flour
80 g/6 tablespoons
golden caster/raw cane
sugar, plus extra for
sprinkling
½ teaspoon baking
powder
½ teaspoon ground
allspice
100 g/7 tablespoons
butter, plus extra for
frying
1 egg
85 g/⅔ cup dried Zante
currants
whole milk, to slacken
(optional)

*a 7-cm/3-inch round
cookie cutter*

Makes about 25

Rub together the flour, sugar, baking powder, allspice and butter in a large mixing bowl.

Add the egg and currants and mix well. Loosen with milk if necessary.

Roll out on a lightly floured work surface to a thickness of 1 cm/⅜ inch. Stamp out rounds using the cookie cutter and set aside.

Put a little butter into a flat grill or frying pan/skillet and set over a low heat. Add the Welsh cakes in batches and gently fry, being careful not to burn them. Turn over and continue to cook.

Leave to cool before sprinkling with a little extra golden caster/raw cane sugar.

NOTE
To make enough Welsh cakes to freeze, simply double or triple the quantities here. Fry the batter and sprinkle with golden caster/raw cane sugar. Once cooled, wrap the Welsh cakes in batches in baking parchment and foil and store in the freezer for up to 2 months. When you want to serve them, simply warm from frozen in a oven preheated to 180°C (350°F) Gas 4 for 5–10 minutes and sprinkle with a little more golden caster/raw cane sugar before serving.

Chocolate and cherry scones
with Kirsch and vanilla Chantilly cream

400 g/3⅓ cups plain/
all-purpose flour
40 g/⅓ cup cocoa
powder, plus extra
for dusting
2½ teaspoons baking
powder
a pinch of salt
100 g/6½ tablespoons
butter, chilled and diced
50 g/¼ cup caster/
granulated sugar
75 g/2½ oz. white
chocolate chips
100 g/¾ cup dried
morello cherries,
roughly chopped
2 egg yolks
250 ml/1 cup whole milk,
plus 1 tablespoon,
to glaze
2 teaspoons lemon juice
cherry jam/jelly (page 11)

KIRSCH AND VANILLA
CHANTILLY CREAM
seeds of ½ vanilla
pod/bean
125 ml/½ cup whipping
cream
125 ml/½ cup double/
heavy cream
25 g/2 tablespoons
caster/superfine sugar
1–2 tablespoons Kirsch,
to taste

*a 5-cm/2-inch round
cookie cutter
a baking sheet lined
with baking parchment*

Makes about 24

These chocolate scones have white chocolate chunks and rehydrated morello cherries in them. I like to serve them with my cherry and Kirsch jam/jelly (page 11), although the first time I made it, I used Amaretto instead of Kirsch which really boosted the cherry flavour. I loved both jams; one was Bakewell-esque and one was Black Forest-esque.

Preheat the oven to 180°C (350°F) Gas 4.

Sift the flour, cocoa powder and baking powder into a large mixing bowl. Add the salt and chilled, diced butter, and start by using a palette knife to cut the butter into the flour, then switch to using your hands to gently rub in the butter. Do not over work the mixture but lift the flour and butter up in your hands and gently press and roll it across your fingertips. When there are no visible pieces of butter remaining add the caster/granulated sugar, white chocolate chips and chopped dried cherries. Mix to combine.

Make a well in the middle of the mixture and add 1 egg yolk, the milk and lemon juice. Use the palette knife to cut the wet ingredients into the dry, then gently mix with your hands until almost combined.

Turn the dough out onto a lightly floured work surface and very gently knead until almost smooth. Pat or roll the dough to a thickness of 3 cm/1¼ inches.

Dip the cookie cutter in flour to prevent it sticking then stamp out discs from the dough and arrange them on the prepared baking sheet. Gather the off-cuts into a ball, re-roll and stamp out more scones.

Mix the remaining egg yolk with 1 tablespoon of milk and neatly brush the top of the scones with the glaze. Bake on the middle shelf of the preheated oven for about 10 minutes until well-risen and golden brown.

To make the Kirsch and vanilla Chantilly cream, put the vanilla seeds in the bowl of a stand mixer or a large mixing bowl (using a handheld electric whisk) and pour over the whipping and double/heavy cream. Add the caster/superfine sugar and beat until soft, billowing peaks form. Add the Kirsch, 1 tablespoon at a time and mix well but be careful not to over-whip the cream or else it will become thick and grainy. Add a little more or less Kirsch to taste.

Serve warm, with cherry jam/jelly and Kirsch and vanilla Chantilly cream spooned on top. Dust with cocoa powder for an extra chocolate hit.

These biscuits are a recipe from the mother of one of my best friends, who says the recipe has been part of her family for generations. A great dunker, these simple ginger biscuits are said to be even better a little underdone just out of the oven… they never normally make it into the cookie jar as they are often scoffed before you get a chance to put them in one.

Veronica's gingerbreads

50 g/3½ tablespoons
    butter
65 g/3½ tablespoons
    margarine
350 g/1¾ cups caster/
    granulated sugar
1 egg, beaten
2–3 teaspoons ground
    ginger
250 g/2 cups self-raising/
    rising flour

*a large baking sheet lined
with baking parchment*

Makes 30

Preheat the oven to 140°C (280°F) Gas 1.

Beat the butter and margarine with the sugar in a large mixing bowl until smooth. Add the beaten egg and mix to combine.

In a separate bowl, sift the ginger into the flour, then add to the wet mixture. Mix to combine – you should end up with a dough similar to shortbread.

Roll into 30 small balls no bigger than a walnut. Arrange on the baking sheet leaving plenty of space between the balls to allow for spreading.

Bake on the middle shelf of the preheated oven for 25–30 minutes. The gingerbreads should remain pale in colour with the texture and appearance of a macaron.

Transfer to a wire rack to cool, then serve.

Golden ginger custard creams

200 g/1¾ sticks butter, softened

125 g/¾ cup plus 2 tablespoons icing/confectioners' sugar

1 teaspoon vanilla extract or vanilla bean paste

2 eggs, lightly beaten

325 g/2½ cups plain/all-purpose flour

25 g/2½ tablespoons cornflour/cornstarch

½ teaspoon baking powder

2 teaspoons ground ginger

½ teaspoon ground cinnamon

¼ teaspoon ground allspice

a grating of fresh nutmeg

a pinch of salt

gold lustre, to decorate

GINGER BUTTERCREAM

125 g/1 stick butter, softened

150 g/1 cup icing/confectioners' sugar

1 teaspoon ground ginger

2 nuggets stem ginger in syrup, drained and finely chopped

a 'Custard Cream' cookie press/stamp (optional)
2 baking sheets lined with baking parchment

Makes 28

One of the ultimate British biscuits, I'd even go as far as to say it's an institution. I managed to find the 'custard cream' cookie press at the Cake International Show in London and have been using it ever since, giving the biscuits my own twist. Spicing up the dough and adding stem ginger to the buttercream gives a lovely wintery twist and spraying them gold with edible lustre makes them very special.

Cream the butter and icing/confectioners' sugar together in a large mixing bowl until really pale and light – this should take about 4 minutes. Add the vanilla extract and mix again. Gradually add the beaten eggs, mixing well between each addition and scraping down the side of the bowl with a rubber spatula. Sift in the flour, cornflour/cornstarch, baking powder, ginger, cinnamon, allspice and nutmeg, and add the salt. Mix again until smooth and thoroughly combined, but do not overwork the dough otherwise the resulting biscuits will be tough rather than crisp. Turn the dough out of the bowl, shape into a ball, flatten into a disc, wrap in clingfilm/plastic wrap and chill in the fridge for at least 4 hours or until firm.

Roll the dough out on a lightly floured work surface to a thickness of around 2 mm/¹⁄₁₆ inch. Press the cookie press/stamp on top of the dough and use the markings to cut out even rectangles. You should be able to cut 56 in total. Arrange the rectangles on the prepared baking sheets leaving a little space between each one. Bring the scraps together, re-roll and stamp to cut out more biscuits. Chill in the fridge for 20 minutes.

Preheat the oven to 170°C (350°F) Gas 4.

Bake on the middle shelf of the preheated oven for about 12 minutes until firm and pale golden brown. Leave to cool on the baking sheets for 2 minutes, then transfer to a wire rack until cold.

Meanwhile prepare the ginger buttercream. Beat the butter until very soft, pale and light – this is easiest using a stand mixer. Gradually add the icing/confectioners' sugar, mixing well between each addition and when it has all been thoroughly incorporated add the ground ginger and chopped stem ginger, and mix again until smooth.

Lay half of the biscuits on the work surface, stamp-side down, and spread with 1 teaspoon of buttercream. Sandwich with the remaining biscuits, gently pressing them together. Brush a little gold lustre on each one to highlight the press and serve.

Treacle tarts *with ginger cake and orange*

One of the best treacle tarts I've ever had was at The Hinds Head, the Michelin starred pub run by one of my culinary mentors Heston Blumenthal. It had crisp pastry with a sweet, buttery and lemony filling. My version uses ginger cake, orange zest and a hint of fresh rosemary for something a little different.

200 g/1²⁄₃ cups plain/
   all-purpose flour
½ teaspoon ground
   ginger
100 g/6½ tablespoons
   butter, chilled and
   diced
a pinch of salt
30 g/4 tablespoons icing/
   confectioners' sugar
1 egg, lightly beaten
2 nuggets of stem ginger
   in syrup, drained and
   finely diced
1 teaspoon orange zest
1 teaspoon finely
   chopped fresh
   rosemary
200 g/7 oz. ginger cake
150 g/²⁄₃ cup golden
   syrup/light corn syrup
1 tablespoon treacle/
   molasses
1 tablespoon orange
   juice
a pinch of salt
1 egg yolk
clotted or double/heavy
   cream, to serve

*12 x 7-cm/3-inch straight-
sided mini tart pans
(or a 12-hole muffin pan)
a 9–10-cm/3½–4-inch
cookie cutter
baking beans (optional)*

Makes 12

Tip the flour into the bowl of the food processor, add the ground ginger, chilled, diced butter and the salt. Pulse to rub the butter into the flour until it is barely visible and sand-like in texture. Add the icing/ confectioners' sugar and pulse to combine. Add the lightly beaten egg and pulse again until the dough starts to come together. Tip the dough out onto the work surface and use your hands to bring it together into a ball but do not over-work the pastry. Flatten into a disc, cover in clingfilm/plastic wrap and chill in the fridge for at least 1 hour until firm.

Roll out the dough on a lightly floured work surface to a thickness of no more than 2 mm/ ¹⁄₁₆ inch. Using the cookie cutter, stamp out 12 discs from the dough. Gently press the pastry discs into the tart pans, trying not to stretch the dough but making sure that the pans are evenly lined. Prick the base of each tart with a fork, arrange the pans on a baking sheet and chill in the fridge for 20 minutes.

Preheat the oven to 170°C (350°F) Gas 3.

Line the tart cases with a square of baking parchment or foil and fill with baking beans or rice. Bake in the preheated oven for 10 minutes until pale golden and starting to crisp. Remove from the oven, lift out the baking beans or rice and parchment or foil and bake for another 1–2 minutes to dry out the bases. Keep the oven on.

Next, prepare the filling. Tip the diced stem ginger into a mixing bowl along with the orange zest and rosemary.

Break the ginger cake into the bowl of a food processor and pulse the cake into crumbs. Tip the crumbs into the bowl with the stem ginger and add the salt.

Pour the golden syrup/light corn syrup, treacle/molasses and orange juice into a small pan and gently warm over a low heat until warm and runny. Pour the syrup into the bowl with the ginger cake and mix to combine. Add the egg yolk and mix again.

Divide the filling evenly between the tart cases – filling them to within 1 mm/¹⁄₁₆ inch from the top of the pastry and bake on the middle shelf of the still warm oven for 14–16 minutes until the filling has set.

Remove from the oven and leave to cool in the pans for 5 minutes before carefully lifting them out onto a wire rack to cool to room temperature before serving with a little scoop of clotted cream or whipped double/heavy cream on top.

Harrods

When it comes to Christmas shopping, the only store to begin with is of course the one and only Harrods. Every year, the famous Knightsbridge store is visited by over 14 million customers, the majority of whom will pass through the food halls. At Christmas, the Harrods chefs produce about 3,000 handmade mince pies, filled with their bespoke Harrods Mincemeat. With hybrids being the fashionable baking trend that they are, brownies, as one of the most luscious and comforting foods ever, are difficult to improve on, unless you add a dash of festive spirit, in the form of mincemeat and a whipped brandy topping.

Mince pie brownies

135 g/1 stick plus 1
  tablespoon butter,
  softened
90 g/¾ cup cocoa
  powder
300 g/1½ cups caster/
  granulated sugar
3 eggs
a pinch of salt
1 teaspoon vanilla extract
95 g/¾ cups plain/
  all-purpose flour
1 teaspoon baking
  powder
200 g/scant 1 cup jarred
  mincemeat
gingerbread men
  sprinkles, to decorate

BRANDY TOPPING
150 g/1 stick plus 2
  tablespoons butter,
  softened
250 g/1¾ cups icing/
  confectioners' sugar
15 ml/1 tablespoon
  brandy

GLAZE
125 g/4 oz. milk/semi-
  sweet chocolate,
  chopped
15 ml/1 tablespoon olive
  oil

a 20 x 30-cm/8 x 12-inch frame or brownie pan, greased and lined with baking parchment

Makes 15

Preheat the oven to 170°C (325°F) Gas 3.

Melt the butter in a heatproof bowl suspended over a pan of barely simmering water and quickly sift in the cocoa powder. Mix to combine then remove from the heat and set aside to cool slightly.

Mix in the sugar and stir until silky smooth. Add the eggs, salt and vanilla extract, and stir in, taking care not to overwork the mixture.

Sift in the flour and baking powder, and fold in using a large metal spoon or rubber spatula. Stir through the mincemeat then pour into the prepared brownie pan. Spread the mixture out evenly then bake in the preheated oven for 25–30 minutes until the top has a light crust but the middle is still soft to the touch.

Remove from the oven and transfer to a wire rack to cool.

To make the brandy topping, beat all the ingredients together until light and fluffy. Spread on top of the cooled brownie and set aside.

To make the glaze, melt the chocolate with the olive oil in a heatproof bowl suspended over a pan of barely simmering water. Stir to remove any lumps and spread on top of the cooled brandy topping. Sprinkle with gingerbread men sprinkles and leave to set.

Using a sharp knife dipped in a little hot water, slice the bownie into slices of about 5 x 8 cm/2 x 3¼ inches.

Hazelnut, apricot and vanilla roulade

These little nutty roulades are perfect for a wintery afternoon tea but can also be served as a large roulade. Filled with a praline-flavoured meringue buttercream, they're light and fluffy, yet indulgent at the same time.

50 g/⅓ cup blanched hazelnuts, plus 150 g/ 1 cup for the topping
100 g/¾ cup plain/ all-purpose flour
1 teaspoon baking powder
½ teaspoon ground ginger
a pinch of salt
5 eggs
140 g/scant ¾ cup caster/ granulated sugar, plus 3 tablespoons for rolling
1 teaspoon vanilla bean paste
zest of 1 lemon
3 tablespoons apricot jam/jelly (page 11)
4 nuggets stem ginger in syrup, drained
1 tablespoon icing/ confectioners' sugar, to dust

HAZELNUT PRALINE
100 g/½ cup caster/ granulated sugar
100 g/⅔ cup hazelnuts, blanched and lightly toasted

MERINGUE BUTTERCREAM
225 g/1 cup plus 2 tablespoons caster/ granulated sugar
4 egg whites
a pinch of salt
250 g/2 sticks butter, softened

a 30 x 40-cm/12 x 16-inch Swiss roll/jellyroll pan, greased, base-lined with baking parchment and lightly floured
a sugar thermometer

Serves 10–12

Preheat the oven to 170°C (325°F) Gas 3.

Tip the hazelnuts into a food processor and finely grind. Add the flour, baking powder, ground ginger and salt, and whizz to combine.

Whisk the eggs and caster/granulated sugar in a stand mixer until pale, trebled in volume and the mixture leaves a ribbon trail when the whisk is lifted from the bowl. Add the vanilla bean paste and lemon zest and mix in.

Using a large metal spoon fold the dry ingredients into the egg and sugar mixture. Gently pour the mixture into the prepared pan and spread level with a palette knife. Bake on the middle shelf of the preheated oven for 12–14 minutes until golden.

Lay a large, clean sheet of baking parchment on the work surface and scatter with 2 tablespoons of caster/granulated sugar.

Remove the cake from the oven and rest for 1 minute before carefully turning it out onto the sugar-coated baking parchment. Peel off the baking parchment from the base of the cake, then roll up the sponge lengthways with the clean side of parchment inside the roll.

While the oven is still on, toast the hazelnuts for the topping on a baking sheet for 3–4 minutes until golden. Leave to cool, then finely chop and set aside until needed.

To make the hazelnut praline, tip the caster/ granulated sugar into a small pan, add 1–2 tablespoons of water and set over a low heat, without stirring, to dissolve the sugar. Bring to the boil and continue to cook until the syrup becomes an amber-coloured caramel, swirling the pan so that it cooks evenly. Tip the toasted nuts into the pan, stir to coat and cook for 30 seconds. Quickly tip the nutty caramel out onto a sheet of baking parchment and leave until hardened and completely cold. Break into chunks and whizz in the food processor until finely chopped. Store in an airtight container until needed.

Make the meringue buttercream following the instructions on page 54 but the quantites listed here. When all of the butter has been incorporated add half of the hazelnut praline, stir to combine and set aside.

Unroll the sponge and, using a palette knife, spread the surface of the cake with the apricot jam/jelly. Spoon one-third of the praline-infused buttercream on top in an even, smooth layer. Scatter the chopped stem ginger over the top of the buttercream, then, using the parchment to help you, roll the sponge back up into a tight roll. Carefully and tightly wrap the roll in clingfilm/plastic wrap and chill in the fridge for 1 hour to firm up.

Unwrap and cover with the remaining buttercream spreading it evenly with a palette knife. Chill again for another 20 minutes to firm up. Scatter the hazelnuts onto a sheet of baking parchment and carefully roll the Swiss roll in the nuts to coat. Dust with icing/ confectioners' sugar and cut into slices.

Strawberry and sherry trifles

100 g/3½ cups amaretti biscuits, lightly crushed
1 tablespoon freeze-dried strawberry powder

STRAWBERRY COMPOTE
350 g/3½ cups strawberries, hulled
100 g/1 cup redcurrants
100 g/½ cup caster/granulated sugar
1–2 teaspoons orange blossom water (optional)

SHERRY CRÈME PATISSIÈRE
350 ml/1⅓ cups whole milk
½ vanilla pod/bean
3 egg yolks
75 g/6½ tablespoons caster/granulated sugar
2 tablespoons cornflour/cornstarch
5 tablespoons sweet sherry

CARAMELIZED ALMONDS
50 g/¼ cup caster/granulated sugar
75 g/1 cup flaked/slivered almonds

WHIPPED CREAM
300 ml/1¼ cups double/heavy cream
1 tablespoon icing/confectioners' sugar
1 teaspoon vanilla bean paste

2 piping/pastry bags fitted with a plain 1-cm/⅜-inch nozzle/tip and a medium star nozzle/tip

Serves 4–6

Now it wouldn't be Christmas without a trifle and this recipe takes the very best of a classic trifle and turns it into a celebratory dessert. Strawberry and redcurrant compote with a little orange blossom flavour is topped with a layer of crushed amaretti biscuits and instead of drenching them in sherry, I infuse my crème pâtissière with the alcohol. With whipped cream on top and finished with a flurry of freeze-dried strawberry powder these little pots of joy are the perfect pud for any celebration.

Slice 250 g/2½ cups of the strawberries and tip into a small pan along with the redcurrants and caster/granulated sugar. Cook over a low heat, stirring frequently until the fruit has cooked down to a jammy consistency. Add the orange blossom water, if using, and dip a teaspoon into the mixture. Allow to cool before tasting, adding more sugar if necessary. Leave to cool, then finely chop the reserved strawberries, add to the compote and chill in the fridge until needed.

To make the sherry crème pâtissière, heat the milk with the vanilla pod/bean in a small pan set over a low heat. Bring slowly just to the boil, then remove from the heat and leave to infuse for 15 minutes. Meanwhile beat the egg yolks with the caster/granulated sugar and cornflour/cornstarch until pale and light. Reheat the milk until just below boiling, then, whisking constantly, pour into the bowl with the egg mixture. Continue mixing until smooth, then return to the pan. Stirring constantly, set the pan over a low–medium heat until the mixture has thickened and is very gently boiling. Add 2 tablespoons of the sherry and strain through a fine mesh sieve/strainer into a clean bowl. Cover the surface with clingfilm/plastic wrap to prevent a skin forming and leave until cold.

To make the caramelized almonds, tip the caster/granulated sugar into a small, non-stick frying pan/skillet, add the flaked/slivered almonds and cook over a low–medium heat, stirring constantly until the sugar has caramelized and the almonds are golden. Tip onto a sheet of baking parchment and leave to cool and harden.

To make the whipped cream, whisk the double/heavy cream with the icing/confectioners' sugar and vanilla bean paste until it will hold soft, floppy peaks. Add 2–3 tablespoons of the whipped cream to the sherry crème pâtissière and fold in using a large metal spoon. Scoop into the piping/pastry bag fitted with the plain nozzle/tip and set aside.

To build the trifles, divide the strawberry compote between the serving glasses and cover with half of the lightly crushed amaretti biscuit. Pipe crème pâtissière over the top and top with another layer of crushed amaretti biscuits.

Spoon the remaining whipped cream into the piping/pastry bag fitted with the star nozzle/tip and pipe swirls on top. Top with the caramelized almonds and a dusting of freeze-dried strawberry powder to serve.

Spiced chocolate domes *with brandy-soaked raisins and cacao nibs*

CACAO NIB DACQUOISE
2 egg whites
75 g/5 tablespoons caster/granulated sugar
25 g/¼ cup ground hazelnuts
40 g/⅓ cup plain/ all-purpose flour
50 g/⅓ cup cacao nibs, plus extra to decorate
½ teaspoon mixed spice/apple pie spice
zest of ½ orange

SOAKED RAISINS
80 g/½ cup (dark) raisins
2 tablespoons dark rum

MOUSSE
125 g/4½ oz. dark/ bittersweet chocolate
60 g/⅓ cup caster/ superfine sugar
400 ml/1⅔ cups whipping cream
1 teaspoon mixed spice/ apple pie spice
½ teaspoon vanilla bean paste

GLAZE
2 g/1 sheet leaf gelatin
250 g/9 oz. dark/ bittersweet chocolate
140 ml/⅔ cup whole milk
50 g/3½ tablespoons liquid glucose
gold leaf, to decorate

a baking sheet lined with baking parchment
a round cookie cutter
a silicone domed chocolate mould

Makes 8–10

Although small and perfectly formed these dainty domes are very rich and delightfully decadent. A rich chocolate mousse filled with brandy-soaked raisins sits atop a cacao nib-studded meringue biscuit.

Preheat the oven to 180°C (350°F) Gas 4.

To make the cacao nib dacquoise base, whisk the egg whites to soft peaks in a mixing bowl with the caster/granulated sugar. In a separate bowl, mix together the ground hazelnuts, flour and cacao nibs, then add the mixed spice/apple pie spice and orange zest. Fold the dry ingredients into the meringue. Spread the mixture onto the prepared baking sheet and bake in the preheated oven for 10 minutes until a skewer inserted into the cake comes out clean. Leave to cool completely before stamping out discs with the cookie cutter.

Put the raisins in a pan with the rum and gently warm over a medium heat. Remove from the heat and leave to cool.

To make the mousse, tip the chopped chocolate into a bowl and set aside. Put the caster/superfine sugar into a pan and cook over a low heat until it begins to caramelize, do not stir the sugar but simply swirl the pan to ensure that it caramelizes evenly. In a separate pan or in a heatproof jug/pitcher in the microwave, heat 125 ml/½ cup of the whipping cream with the mixed spice/apple pie spice and vanilla bean paste and slowly bring to the boil. Meanwhile whip the remaining cream to soft peaks and set aside in a cool place. When the sugar has turned golden, slide the pan off the heat and gradually pour the hot cream into the caramel – be very careful as it will splatter.

Stir constantly with a long handled wooden spoon until smooth. Pour the caramel cream over the chopped chocolate and mix gently until melted and smooth.

Leave the chocolate caramel cream to cool for 10 minutes and then fold through the whipped cream. Spoon into the moulds and using the back of the spoon spread up the sides of the mould to create a border. Fill with the soaked raisins, put a little more mousse in before pressing a disc of the cacao nib dacqoise down to create the base. Clean up any excess mousse and make sure they are level. Freeze overnight.

To make the glaze, soften the gelatin in a bowl of cold water for 10 minutes. Put the chocolate in a mixing bowl. Pour the milk, 60 ml/¼ cup of water and liquid glucose into a pan and bring to the boil over a low heat, stirring to combine. Remove the pan from the heat, drain the gelatin from the cold water and drop into the hot milk. Whisk to combine, then pour over the chocolate, leave for 2 minutes, then stir gently with a rubber spatula until smooth and glossy. Leave to cool for a further 2 minutes. Remove the frozen domes from their moulds and place on a cooling rack over a tray. Pour over the glaze and tap the rack gently to remove excess. Leave to cool before using a palette knife to transfer to a plate. Decorate the bottoms with cacao nibs and the tops with gold leaf.

Beetroot cured salmon *with horseradish crème fraîche on rye bread*

Chicken liver parfait *with thyme and onion confit and fluted brioche*

Roasted walnut and miso shortbread

Earl Grey and lemon teapots

Rhubarb and custard macarons

Apple crumble and custard tartlets

Coffee and caramel éclairs

Dark chocolate and yuzu teacakes

Buttermilk panna cotta *with strawberry compote and orange crumble*

Belmond Le Manoir aux Quat'Saisons Apricot and lavender almondine

Strawberry and Champagne tarts

Matcha tea, lime and almond friands

Something special

Beetroot cured salmon *with horseradish crème fraîche on rye bread*

a 500-g/18-oz. piece of
salmon, pin-boned
and scaled (skin on)
1 tablespoon grated
fresh or preserved
horseradish
175 g/¾ cup crème
fraîche
6–8 thin slices rye bread
50 g/3½ tablespoons
butter
salt and freshly ground
black pepper, to taste
fresh dill or watercress,
to garnish

BEETROOT/BEET CURE
2 raw beetroot/beets
(about 200 g/7 oz.)
1 teaspoon pink
peppercorns
1 teaspoon fennel seeds
1 teaspoon juniper
berries
60 g/⅓ cup coarse sea
salt
50 g/¼ cup golden
caster/raw cane sugar
zest of 1 lemon
zest of ½ orange
2–3 tablespoons freshly
chopped dill
3 tablespoons vodka

*a baking sheet lined with
three layers of clingfilm/
plastic wrap*

Makes 18–20

Curing your own salmon for a celebration really isn't as difficult as it may sound! It gives you such satisfaction when it is done and tastes amazing. The colour of the beetroot doesn't quite seep into the centre of the salmon giving you such a lovely colour contrast. The delicate flavour of the dill, with the pink peppercorns and vodka really come through too.

First, prepare the beetroot/beet cure. Peel and coarsely grate the beetroot/beets into a large mixing bowl. Lightly crush the peppercorns, fennel seeds and juniper berries using a pestle and mortar, applying just enough pressure to release their flavours. Add them to the bowl with the salt, sugar, lemon and orange zests and half of the chopped dill. Mix to combine.

Scatter one-third of the beetroot/beet cure over the prepared baking sheet and lay the salmon on top, skin-side down. Cover the salmon with the remaining cure, pressing it into an even layer over the fish. Slowly spoon the vodka over the top and wrap the salmon tightly in the excess clingfilm/plastic wrap. Lay another tray or tin on top of the salmon and weigh it down with something heavy. Set in the fridge for at least 2 days to cure.

Take the salmon from the fridge and unwrap it over a sink to catch the purple juices. Using your hands, scrape off as much of the beetroot/beet cure as possible and pat the fish dry with paper towels. Finely chop the remaining dill and press into the top (flesh side) of the salmon. Using a very sharp knife cut the salmon into wafer thin slices – cutting down to, but not through the skin so you can transfer it easily to a serving platter.

Mix the grated horseradish with the crème fraîche and salt and black pepper. Thinly spread the rye bread slices with butter and cut into bite-sized pieces. Spread with the horseradish crème fraîche and lay the salmon slices on top. Garnish with a little fresh dill or watercress and a twist of freshly ground black pepper. Caper berries work exceptionally well with this tartine, too.

Chicken liver parfait *with thyme and onion confit and fluted brioche*

CHICKEN LIVER PARFAIT
200 g/1²/₃ sticks butter
1 tablespoon olive oil
2 garlic cloves, crushed
3 shallots, finely chopped
1 sprig fresh thyme, leaves picked
a pinch of freshly grated nutmeg
3 tablespoons Madeira
500 g/18 oz. chicken livers, trimmed
salt and freshly ground black pepper, to taste

BRIOCHE
250 g/2 cups strong white bread flour
25 g/2 tablespoons caster/granulated sugar
5 g/1 teaspoon fast-action dried yeast
a pinch of salt
3 eggs
125 g/1 stick butter, diced and softened
2 tablespoons whole milk

ONION CONFIT
3 small onions, finely sliced
1 tablespoon olive oil
25 g/1½ tablespoons butter
1 sprig fresh thyme, leaves picked
1½ tablespoon golden caster/raw cane sugar
2 tablespoons cider vinegar

a piping/pastry bag fitted with a star nozzle/tip
12 brioche pans, greased

Serves 12

I love pâté on toast as a snack, but when chicken liver parfait is piped on top of buttery brioche like a cupcake frosting, it takes things to a whole new level. Serve cornichons on the side to cut through the richness of the dish.

For the parfait, heat 25 g/1¾ tablespoons of the butter and half of the olive oil in a frying pan/skillet, add the shallots and the thyme leaves, season with salt and black pepper and cook over a low–medium heat until the shallots are tender but not coloured. Add the garlic and nutmeg, and cook for a further minute. Add the Madeira and cook, stirring, until the liquid has evaporated. Remove from the pan and scoop into a food processor.

Wipe out the pan and return to a medium–high heat with the remaining olive oil and a further 25 g/1¾ tablespoons butter. When the butter is foaming, add half the chicken livers and cook until just cooked through but still pink in the middle – no more than 2 minutes. Transfer to the food processor. Cook the remaining chicken livers in the same pan, add to the processor and whizz until smooth.

Dice 150 g/1 stick plus 2½ tablespoons of the remaining butter and gradually add it to the mixer with the motor running. Next, push the parfait mixture through a fine mesh sieve/strainer, taste and season with salt and black pepper. Spoon into the piping/pastry bag and leave until cold. Cover and chill in the fridge until needed.

To make the brioche, tip the flour, sugar, yeast and salt into the bowl of a stand mixer fitted with a dough hook. Mix, then make a well. Add the eggs and mix to combine. Gradually add the butter, mixing slowly and steadily until the dough is silky smooth and elastic. Cover with clingfilm/plastic wrap and leave for 1–2 hours until doubled in size.

Meanwhile, prepare the onion confit. Tip the sliced onions into a pan with the olive oil and butter. Add the thyme leaves, season with salt and black pepper, and cook over a low heat, stirring frequently, until the onions are tender and starting to turn golden – do not rush this stage. Add the sugar and vinegar and continue to cook for a further 10 minutes until the onions are sticky and starting to caramelize. Remove from the pan and leave to cool before covering until ready to use.

Tip the brioche dough out onto a lightly floured work surface, knead gently for 30 seconds, then divide the dough into 12 even-sized balls. Transfer to the brioche pans and arrange on a baking sheet. Cover loosely with clingfilm/plastic wrap and leave for 45 minutes–1 hour.

Preheat the oven to 190°C (375°F) Gas 5.

Brush the top of each brioche with milk and bake on the middle shelf of the preheated oven for about 20 minutes until golden brown and the buns sound hollow when tapped on the bottoms. Remove from the pans and leave to cool on a wire rack.

Top each brioche with a little onion confit and finish with a swirl of parfait.

These little shortbread biscuits, flavoured with miso and rolled in chopped walnuts before baking, work perfectly as a sweet or savoury biscuit. Try them sandwiched with a miso and chocolate ganache or with some cheese and chutney; either way they're delicious.

Roasted walnut and miso shortbread

250 g/2 sticks plus butter, softened

75 g/4½ tablespoons white or barley miso

150 g/¾ cup golden caster/raw cane sugar, plus extra for sprinkling

½ teaspoon vanilla bean paste

300 g/2⅓ cups plain/all-purpose flour

100 g/⅔ cup wholegrain rye or spelt flour

½ teaspoon baking powder

a pinch of salt

100 g/¾ cup walnut pieces

2 tablespoons whole milk

2 baking sheets lined with baking parchment

Makes 35–40

Tip the butter and miso paste into the bowl of a stand mixer, add the sugar and mix for 3–4 minutes until the mixture is pale and light. Add the vanilla bean paste and mix again to combine.

Sift the flours, baking powder and a pinch of salt into the bowl and mix again until smooth and thoroughly combined but do not overwork the dough.

Tip the dough out onto the work surface and shape into two neat logs each with a diameter of about 5 cm/2 inches. Wrap tightly in clingfilm/plastic wrap and chill for at least 4 hours or overnight.

Preheat the oven to 170°C (325°F) Gas 3.

Finely chop the walnuts and tip into a baking tray in a smooth layer. Unwrap the dough logs and brush the surface of each with milk to coat. Roll the dough logs in the finely chopped walnuts so that they are completely coated in an even layer of walnuts. Using a sharp knife, cut each log into slices 3–5 mm/⅛–¼ inch thick and arrange on the prepared baking sheets, leaving a little space between each shortbread. Sprinkle with a sugar and bake on the middle shelf of the preheated oven for 12–15 minutes until golden.

Leave to cool on the baking sheets for 2 minutes and then transfer to a wire rack until cold before serving.

What's more British that a cup of tea and a biscuit? Well I've combined those two, with my Earl Grey-infused lemon biscuits cut in the shape of a teapot! I've created the texture on the icing with a textured rolling mat. You can find really elaborately designed ones in good cake decorating shops or online.

Earl Grey and lemon teapots

4 teaspoons loose Earl Grey tea leaves
200 g/1¾ sticks butter, softened
175 g/¾ cup plus 2 tablespoons golden caster/raw cane sugar
zest of 1 lemon
1 teaspoon vanilla extract
1 egg, lightly beaten
a few drops of food-grade bergamot oil (optional)
425 g/3⅓ cups plain/all-purpose flour
1 teaspoon baking powder
a pinch of salt
icing/confectioners' sugar, for rolling out
400 g/14 oz. coloured sugarpaste icing/frosting
lustre dust, to decorate (optional)

a teapot-shaped cookie cutter
2 baking sheets lined with baking parchment
a textured silicon rolling mat (optional)

Makes about 24

Tip the Earl Grey tea leaves into a mortar and gently grind with the pestle; they should retain a little texture. If the leaves are too finely ground they will make the shortbreads a grey colour.

Cream together the butter and sugar until pale and light. Add the tea leaves and lemon zest and mix again. Gradually add the egg in two or three additions and mix until thoroughly combined.

Sift together the flour, baking powder and salt into the bowl and continue mixing until combined. Bring the dough together into a ball using your hands, flatten into a disc, wrap in clingfilm/plastic wrap and chill for 2 hours or until firm.

Roll the dough out on a lightly floured work surface to a thickness of around 3 mm/⅛ inch and use the teapot-shaped cookie cutter to stamp out shapes from the dough and arrange on the lined baking sheets. Gather the dough off-cuts and re-roll to make more shapes and chill the biscuits for a further 30 minutes.

Preheat the oven to 170°C (325°F) Gas 3.

Bake the biscuits on the middle shelf of the preheated oven for about 12 minutes until lightly golden and firm to the touch. Leave to cool on the sheets for 2 minutes and then transfer to a wire rack until cold.

Lightly dust the work surface with icing/confectioners' sugar and roll out the sugarpaste in the colour of your choice to a thickness of about 2 mm/¹⁄₁₆ inch. Lay the textured mat if using on top and give another couple of turns of the rolling pin to press the indents into the icing. Using the cookie cutter, stamp out a shape from the icing/frosting, lightly brush one biscuit with water and lay the icing/frosting shape neatly on top. Gently press the two together and repeat until all of the biscuits are covered. Using a clean paint brush, decorate each biscuit with lustre if you wish. Leave to dry out before serving.

One of my all time favourite flavour combinations! I don't know whether it is rhubarb crumble with custard or those classic boiled sweets/hard candies that are to blame. Either way, these double-filled macarons certainly make me feel 'all warm inside'! You could also use other winning pairings such as strawberries and cream or raspberry and lemon... so many possibilities.

Rhubarb and custard macarons

175 g/1¾ cups ground almonds
175 g/1¼ cups icing/confectioners' sugar
150 g/scant ¾ cup egg whites (about 4 egg whites)
200 g/1 cup caster/superfine sugar
1 teaspoon vanilla extract
pink food colouring paste
4 tablespoons rhubarb jam/jelly (page 14)
red food colouring, to decorate

BUTTERCREAM
150 g/1 stick plus 2 tablespoons butter, softened
300 g/2 cups icing/confectioners' sugar
1 teaspoon custard powder
1 teaspoon vanilla extract

2 large baking sheets lined with baking parchment
a 4-cm/1½-inch plain cookie cutter
a large piping/pastry bag fitted with a 1-cm/⅜-inch plain nozzle/tip
2 disposable piping/pastry bags

Makes 30

Using the cookie cutter as a guide, draw 30 evenly spaced circles in neat lines on each piece of baking parchment, leaving a little space between each circle. Flip the paper over – the pencil lines should show through – and place one piece on each baking sheet.

Combine the ground almonds and icing/confectioners' sugar in a food processor and blitz for up to 1 minute to finely grind and thoroughly mix. Tip into a mixing bowl, add 50 g/scant ¼ cup of the egg whites and beat until combined into a thick paste. Set aside.

Fill a medium-sized saucepan with water and bring to a gentle simmer. Tip the remaining egg whites into a medium heatproof bowl, add the caster/superfine sugar and set the bowl over the simmering water, ensuring that it does not touch the water. Slowly beat the egg whites and sugar with a handheld electric whisk until combined, continuing to whisk for about 3 minutes until the sugar has completely dissolved and the mixture is a thick glossy, bright white meringue. Remove the bowl from the pan and continue to whisk on medium–fast speed for another 3 minutes until cool and very thick. With a large metal spoon or rubber spatula, fold in the vanilla and food colouring in tiny amounts – you can add more but you can't take any away.

Add one-quarter of the meringue to the almond paste, stirring well to loosen and combine the mixture. Fold this back into the meringue and mix until well combined and resembling thick molten lava that will hold a ribbon trail for about 5 seconds.

Working quickly, scoop the mixture into a large piping/pastry bag and pipe 30 even-sized macarons onto each baking sheet using the circles as a guide. Set aside for about 30 minutes until the macarons have firmed up and a light skin has formed on the surface.

Preheat the oven to 160°C (325°F) Gas 3.

Bake the macarons, one sheet at a time, on the middle shelf of the preheated oven for 10–12 minutes until well risen and crisp on top. Remove and allow to cool completely on the sheets.

Meanwhile, prepare the buttercream filling. Beat the butter until really pale and light. Gradually add the icing/confectioners' sugar in 3 or 4 batches and mix until smooth. Add the custard powder and vanilla extract and combine thoroughly. Scoop the buttercream into a disposable piping/pastry bag and snip the end into a ½–1 cm/¼–½ inch nozzle.

Turn half of the macarons upside down and pipe the buttercream in a ring around the edge of the flat surface. Fill the hole in the middle of the ring with rhubarb jam/jelly and sandwich with the remaining macaron shells. Brush with red food colouring and serve.

Apple crumble and custard tartlets

1 quantity pastry
(page 103)

CRUMBLE
50 g/⅓ cup plus
1 tablespoon plain/
all-purpose flour
50 g/½ cup ground
almonds
50 g/¼ cup caster/
granulated sugar
50 g/3½ tablespoons
butter, chilled and
diced

APPLE MOUSSE
2 Bramley or other tart
apples, peeled, cored
and chopped
3 crisp eating apples
3 tablespoons caster/
granulated sugar
25 g/1½ tablespoons
butter
1 tablespoon lemon juice
1 cinnamon stick
3 sheets platinum-grade
leaf gelatin
2 egg yolks
150 ml/⅔ cup double/
heavy cream

GLAZE
5 sheets platinum-grade
leaf gelatin
300 ml/1¼ cups apple
juice

*a 9–10-cm/3½–4-inch
cookie cutter
a 12-hole muffin pan
baking beans (optional)
a baking sheet lined
with baking parchment
a domed silicon cake-pop
mould*

Makes 12

One of our most beloved puds given patisserie pampering! Using brilliant and simple ingredients, with a touch of special moulding and of course some sparkle, this takes apple crumble and custard to a whole new level!

Roll out the pastry on a lightly floured work surface to a thickness of no more than 2 mm/ ¹⁄₁₆ inch. Using the cookie cutter, stamp out 12 discs. Gently press the pastry discs into the prepared tart pans, trying not to stretch the dough until evenly lined. Prick the bases with a fork and arrange on a baking sheet and chill in the fridge for 20 minutes.

Preheat the oven to 170°C (325°F) Gas 3.

Line the holes of the muffin pan with baking parchment or foil and fill with baking beans or rice. Bake in the preheated oven for 10 minutes until pale golden and starting to crisp. Remove the baking beans or rice and parchment or foil and bake for 1–2 minutes to dry out the bases.

To make the crumble, tip all the ingredients into the bowl of a food processor and pulse until the butter has been rubbed in and the mixture starts to clump together. Tip onto the prepared baking sheet and bake on the middle shelf of the still hot oven for about 10 minutes until golden and crisp. Leave to cool.

To make the apple mousses, tip the chopped apple into a saucepan with the sugar, butter, lemon juice and cinnamon. Cover with a disc of baking parchment and a lid, and cook over a low–medium heat for about 20 minutes or until the apples have reduced. Stir several times to prevent sticking. Remove from the heat and spoon one-third of the compote into a small bowl and set aside. Pass the

remaining compote through a fine mesh sieve/strainer into a bowl. Taste and add a little more sugar if tart.

Soak the gelatin leaves in a bowl of cold water for 5 minutes until soft and floppy. Beat the egg yolks into the hot, smooth apple purée and add the drained gelatin leaves. Beat until thoroughly combined. Set aside to cool, then chill for 30 minutes to thicken up slightly.

Meanwhile, whip the cream until just firm and fold into the chilled purée to form a mousse. Spoon into a piping/pastry bag and pipe into the domed silicon mould. Pop in the freezer for 45 minutes to firm up.

To make the glaze, soften the gelatin leaves in a bowl of cold water for 5 minutes. Heat half of the apple juice in a small saucepan until just below boiling. Drain the gelatin from the water, drop into the hot apple juice and whisk to melt. Add the cold apple juice and mix to combine. Chill in the fridge for 15 minutes until starting to thicken.

Turn the nearly frozen mousse out of the moulds onto a clean sheet of baking parchment and carefully spoon over the cold jelly to coat in an even thin layer. Chill in the fridge for 10 minutes.

Divide the reserved apple compote between the baked pastry cases. Carefully lift one jelly-coated mousse onto each tart and scatter the crumble around the edges.

There is something so elegant and sophisticated about little pastries, as epitomised by these caramel-cream-filled, coffee iced eclairs! The flavours work well together as the caramel balances out the intensity of the coffee.

Coffee and caramel éclairs

75 ml/5 tablespoons whole milk

60 g/4 tablespoons butter, diced

a pinch of salt

a pinch of sugar

100 g/¾ cup plain/ all-purpose flour, sifted

3 eggs, lightly beaten

CARAMEL

150 g/¾ cup caster/ granulated sugar

100 ml/⅓ cup whipping cream

25 g/1½ tablespoons unsalted butter

a pinch of sea salt flakes

TO DECORATE

225 g/1⅔ cups fondant icing/confectioners' sugar

2 teaspoons instant coffee granules

75 g/2½ oz. chopped dark/bittersweet chocolate, melted

coffee beans (optional)

a large baking sheet lined with baking parchment
2 disposable piping/ pastry bags
a piping/pastry bag fitted with a star nozzle/tip

Makes about 30

Preheat the oven to 180°C (350°F) Gas 4.

Put 75 ml/5 tablespoons of water in a medium saucepan with the milk and butter and set over a medium heat. Stir constantly to melt the butter. As soon as the mixture comes to the boil, reduce the heat slightly and, working quickly and keeping the pan over a low heat, stir in the flour and season well with salt and black pepper. Beat vigorously until smooth and the mixture cleanly leaves the sides of the pan – this will take about 2 minutes.

Transfer the dough to a stand mixer or mixing bowl (using a handheld electric whisk) and gradually beat in the eggs 1 tablespoon at a time. You might not need all of the egg – when the dough is soft and smooth and drops off a spoon leaving a 'V' shape behind it is ready. Scoop the dough into the piping/ pastry bag and pipe 30 éclairs onto the prepared baking sheets leaving plenty of space between each one. Bake on the middle shelves of the preheated oven for 10–15 minutes until well-risen, golden brown and sound hollow in the middle when tapped. Remove from the oven and make a small hole in the side of each bun with a skewer and return to the oven for a further 1 minute to dry out the insides. Leave to cool on a wire rack until cold.

To make the caramel, tip the sugar into a medium saucepan. Add 1 tablespoon of water and set the pan over a low–medium heat to dissolve the sugar, without stirring. Continue to cook the syrup until it becomes an amber-coloured caramel, swirling the pan to ensure the caramel cooks evenly. Meanwhile, heat 100 ml/⅓ cup of the cream until it just boils either in a heatproof jug/pitcher in the microwave or in a small saucepan. Working quickly, slide the caramel off the heat and carefully add the hot cream (the caramel will hiss and bubble). Add the butter and salt, nd stir until smooth. Return the pan to a low heat, simmer for 30 seconds, then strain.

Next, prepare the fondant glaze for decoration. Sift the fondant icing/confectioners' sugar into a bowl. In another small bowl dissolve the coffee granules in 2 teaspoons of boiling water. Add the coffee to the sugar and, whisking constantly, add enough cold water to make a soft, smooth spreadable glaze. Cover and set aside.

When you are ready to fill the éclairs, whip the remaining cream until it will hold a soft peak. Fold 2–3 tablespoons of cream into the reserved caramel to lighten it and then carefully fold in the rest. Spoon into the piping/pastry bag. Cut each éclair in half and pipe the caramel cream into the bottom half, then cover with the lid. Using a teaspoon or small off-set palette knife, spread the fondant glaze neatly over the top of each éclair and leave for about 30 minutes to set.

Drizzle melted chocolate over each éclair, decorate with a coffee bean and serve.

For me, there is something very nostalgic and comforting about biting through crisp chocolate into a fluffy, sticky marshmallow and a crumbly base. We used to have them as kids as a treat for being good. Store-bought teacakes seem terribly sweet to me nowadays, so I've added lemon to my marshmallow and a lime and yuzu curd to create something more sophisticated.

Dark chocolate and yuzu teacakes

50 g/3½ tablespoons
   butter, softened
40 g/scant ¼ cup caster/
   granulated sugar
1 egg yolk
1 teaspoon lemon zest
80 g/⅔ cup plain/
   all-purpose flour
a pinch of baking
   powder
a pinch of salt
12–16 teaspoons lime
   and yuzu curd (page 12)

MARSHMALLOW TOPPING
3 sheets platinum-grade
   leaf gelatin
125 g/scant ⅔ cup
   caster/superfine sugar
zest and juice of 1 lemon
2 egg whites
a pinch of salt

TO DECORATE
200 g/6½ oz. chopped
   dark/bittersweet
   chocolate, chopped
edible gold powder

a 5-cm/2-inch plain
cookie cutter
a baking sheet lined
with baking parchment
a sugar thermometer
a large piping/pastry bag
fitted with a plain 1-cm/
⅜-inch nozzle/tip

Makes 12–16

Start by making the biscuit bases. Tip the butter and caster sugar into a medium sized bowl and using a rubber spatula cream them together until pale and light. Add the egg yolk and lemon zest and mix again until thoroughly combined. Sift the flour and baking powder into the bowl, add the salt and mix again until smooth, but do not overwork the dough. Gather the dough into a ball, flatten into a disc, cover with clingfilm/plastic wrap and chill for 30 minutes.

Roll the chilled dough out on a lightly floured work surface to a thickness of around 3 mm/ ⅛ inch. Using the cutter stamp out 12–16 discs and arrange on the baking sheet. Chill again for 20 minutes while you preheat the oven to 170°C (350°F) Gas 3. Prick each biscuit with a fork and bake on the middle shelf for 12 minutes until pale golden brown. Leave to cool on the baking sheet and then top with a scant teaspoon of lime and yuzu curd.

Next, prepare the marshmallow topping. Put the gelatin in a bowl of cold water and set aside for 10 minutes to soften and soak. Tip the sugar and lemon juice into a small pan, add 50 ml/3½ tablespoons water and set the pan over a low heat to dissolve the sugar. Bring the syrup to the boil and continue to cook until it reaches 120°C (248°F) on a sugar thermometer. Meanwhile, tip the egg whites into the bowl of a stand mixer fitted with a

whisk attachment and add the salt. As soon as the syrup reaches the correct temperature slide the pan off the heat and working quickly remove the thermometer and start to whisk the egg whites on a fast speed until they will hold a soft peak. With the motor running on a low speed, slowly and carefully pour the hot syrup into the bowl. Remove the soft gelatin leaves from the water, squeeze out any excess water, blot briefly on kitchen paper and add to the meringue mixture. Turn the mixer up to high speed again and continue mixing until the marshmallow is cool, very thick, glossy white and will hold a very firm peak. Add the lemon zest and mix to combine.

Working quickly, scoop the marshmallow into the prepared piping bag and pipe a generous mound on top of each biscuit completely encasing the curd. Leave to set for at least 1 hour.

Temper the chocolate by melting in the microwave in bursts of 30 seconds. Once the mixture is three-quarters melted, stop heating and stir well to remove any lumps. Dip one marshmallow-covered biscuit at a time into the melted chocolate to completely cover the marshmallow. Place on a wire rack set over a tray to catch any drips and repeat to cover all the teacakes. Leave the chocolate to harden slightly or completely, then dust with edible gold powder.

Buttermilk panna cotta *with strawberry compote and orange crumble*

4 sheets platinum-grade leaf gelatin
1 vanilla pod/bean
450 ml/1¾ cups double/heavy cream
80 g/5 tablespoons caster/superfine sugar
450 ml/1¾ cups buttermilk

ORANGE CRUMBLE
50 g/3½ tablespoons butter, chilled and diced
50 g/¼ cup caster/granulated sugar
75 g/scant ⅔ cup plain/all-purpose flour
25 g/¼ cup ground almonds
1 teaspoon orange zest

STRAWBERRY COMPOTE
250 g/2½ cups strawberries, hulled
1 tablespoon caster/granulated sugar
juice of ½ orange
½ teaspoon orange zest
icing/confectioners' sugar, for dusting

12 shot glasses or similar small dishes
a baking sheet lined with baking parchment

Makes 12

The buttermilk in these panna cottas give a really delicate flavour but it's the texture I adore. Sometimes a panna cotta made with only double/heavy cream can be too heavy and claggy; the buttermilk somehow lightens the finished cream. With a fragrant strawberry compote and crunchy orange crumble, it's a lovely little dessert to help cleanse your palette after your scones.

Place the gelatin leaves in a bowl of cold water and leave to soak for 5 minutes until soft and floppy.

Cut the vanilla pod/bean in half and scrape out the black seeds using the point of a small knife. Place the vanilla pod/bean and seeds into a saucepan with the cream and sugar. Set the pan over a medium heat and bring slowly to the boil. Remove from the heat and set aside for 5 minutes to allow the vanilla to infuse the mixture.

Bring the cream back to the boil and remove from the heat. Drain the gelatin leaves from the water and squeeze out any excess water. Add to the hot cream and whisk well to ensure that the gelatin dissolves evenly. Add the buttermilk, mix to combine and strain into a jug/pitcher.

Pour the panna cotta mixture into the shot glasses, cool and then cover with clingfilm/plastic wrap and chill for at least 4 hours or until set.

Prepare the crumble while the panna cotta is chilling. Preheat the oven to 170°C (325°F) Gas 3. Tip all of the ingredients into the bowl of a food processor and pulse until the butter has been rubbed into the dry ingredients and the mixture starts to clump together. Tip onto the baking sheet and bake on the middle shelf of the oven for about 15 minutes until crisp and golden. Leave to cool.

To make the compote, slice the strawberries and tip into a bowl. Add the sugar, orange juice and zest and mix gently to combine. Cover and leave to one side for 30 minutes to allow the strawberries to soften slightly and become juicy. Spoon the strawberry compote on top of the set panna cottas and top with a teaspoon of crumble. Dust with icing/confectioners' sugar to serve.

This recipe comes from Benoit Blin MCA, who is Head Pastry Chef at Raymond Blanc's Belmond Le Manoir aux Quat' Saisons, and one of the most excellent and well respected pâtissiers I've worked with. For over 20 years, he has been able to source produce such as the apricots he poaches for this recipe, from the organic restaurant gardens, but here I use canned apricots.

Apricot and lavender almondine

150 g/5½ oz. shortcrust pastry, rolled 2-mm/¹⁄₁₆-inch thick, and cut into 10 x 7-cm/3-inch discs
10 canned apricot halves

ALMOND CREAM
110 g/1 cup plus 1 tablespoon ground almonds
110 g/¾ cup icing/confectioners' sugar
7 g/2 teaspoons cornflour/cornstarch
110 g/1 stick butter, softened
2 eggs
1 teaspoon vanilla extract

CRUMBLE
40 g/⅓ cup plain/all-purpose flour (T55)
25 g/2 tablespoons butter
25 g/2 tablespoons caster/superfine sugar
10 g/1 tablespoon demerara/turbinado sugar

APRICOT & LAVENDER GLAZE
250 g/1 cup homemade apricot jam/jelly (page 11)
4 fresh garden lavender flower heads

FOR THE PRALINETTES
80 g/1 cup nibbed almonds
60 g/scant ⅓ cup caster/superfine sugar

a large piping/pastry bag fitted with a plain 1-cm/³⁄₈-inch nozzle/tip
a sugar thermometer
10 stainless steel rings (7-cm/3-inch diameter, 2-cm/1-inch deep), greased and lined with a band of baking parchment

Makes 10

First make the almond cream. Combine the dry ingredients in a bowl. Put the butter in a stand mixer, beat in the dry ingredients and slowly incorporate the eggs and the vanilla extract. Mix well and reserve in the piping/pastry bag.

Next, put all the crumble ingredients into a large mixing bowl and work together with fingertips to the consistency of breadcrumbs. Spread onto a baking sheet and freeze. Blitz in a food processor from frozen, then store in the freezer until needed.

Put the apricot jam/jelly for the glaze in a pan with the lavender and warm to about 50°C (122°F) on a sugar thermometer. Whisk well, then cover with cling film/plastic wrap to infuse for 45 minutes. Blitz in the food processor for 10 seconds to break up the flowers and reserve until needed.

To make the pralinettes, bring the sugar and 2 teaspoons water to 115°C (240°F). Add in the nuts and stir with a spatula. Allow the sugar to crystallize around the nuts, gently stirring. Turn onto a cold baking sheet to cool completely.

Preheat the oven to 170°C (325°F) Gas 3.

To assemble, pat dry the apricot halves with paper towels. Arrange the rings on a baking sheet with a silicon mat and place a pastry disc inside each ring. Pipe about 35 g/1¼ oz. of almond cream into each ring. Place an apricot half in the centre of each one, sliced-side down, and sprinkle the crumble generously around the edges. Bake in the preheated oven for 30–35 minutes. Remove the rings from around the almondines and allow them to cool.

Reheat the apricot and lavender glaze and brush it over the top of each apricot. Sprinkle the pralinettes all around the edge of the apricots and dust with icing/confectioners' sugar.

Strawberry and Champagne tarts

100 g/6½ tablespoons butter, softened
50 g/⅓ cup icing/confectioners' sugar
a pinch of salt
1 egg, lightly beaten
1 teaspoon vanilla bean paste
175 g/1⅓ cups plain/all-purpose flour

CRÈME PÂTISSIÈRE
1 vanilla pod/bean
150 ml/⅔ cup whipping cream
125 ml/½ cup Champagne
50 g/¼ cup caster/superfine sugar
2 egg yolks
1½ tablespoons cornflour/cornstarch
1 tablespoon butter

TO DECORATE
400 g/4 cups strawberries, hulled
4 tablespoons apricot jam/jelly (page 11)
edible gold leaf (optional)

a 8–9-cm/3¼–3½-inch round cookie cutter
12 x 7-cm/3-inch mini tart pans or a 12-hole muffin pan
baking beans (optional)

Makes 12

Afternoon tea just isn't complete without a strawberry tart! It is classically filled with a vanilla crème pâtissière, and here I've made mine with Champagne (Prosecco will work well, too) to make the tart even more decadent. Add a simple apricot glaze and a touch of gold leaf and you'll think you're taking tea in a 5-star hotel!

Start by making the pastry. Cream the butter, sugar and salt together in a stand mixer or in a bowl with a handheld electric whisk until pale – this will take 3–4 minutes.

With the mixer running, gradually add the egg with the vanilla bean paste, mixing until fully incorporated. Gently mix in the flour but do not overwork the dough. Bring the dough together into a ball, wrap in clingfilm/plastic wrap, flatten into a disc and chill for at least 2 hours or until needed.

Roll out the pastry on a lightly floured work surface to a thickness of no more than 2 mm/1/16 inch. Stamp out discs from the dough using the cookie cutter. Neatly line the tart pans with the pastry discs and trim off any excess with a small sharp knife. Prick the bases with a fork, line with a square of baking parchment or foil and fill with baking beans or rice. Arrange the pans on a baking sheet and chill in the fridge for 20 minutes.

Preheat the oven to 180°C (350°F) Gas 4.

Bake the pastry cases on the middle shelf of the preheated oven for about 10–12 minutes or until pale golden. Remove the baking beans or rice and parchment or foil and continue to cook for 1 minute until the bases are crisp. Remove from the oven and cool. Remove the cases and arrange on a tray.

Prepare the crème pâtissière. Cut the vanilla pod/bean in half down its length and pop into a small saucepan. Add the cream and Champagne and bring slowly to the boil over a low heat. Combine the sugar, egg yolks and cornflour/cornstarch in a mixing bowl and beat until pale and smooth. As soon as the cream mixture comes to the boil remove it from the heat and pour half into the mixing bowl, whisking constantly until smooth. Using a rubber spatula, scoop the mixture back into the pan and return to a low heat, stirring constantly until the crème pâtissière just starts to boil and thickens quite considerably.

Slide the pan off the heat, remove the vanilla pod/bean, add the butter and mix until combined. Divide the crème patissierie between the pastry cases and spread level. Leave to cool for 10 minutes.

Quarter the strawberries and arrange on top of the crème pâtissière. Warm the apricot jam/jelly – either in a small pan over a low heat or in the microwave in short bursts. Pass through a fine mesh sieve/strainer to remove any lumps and gently brush over the top of the strawberries. Decorate each tart with a piece of gold leaf if you wish and leave for 30 minutes or so to allow the jam/jelly to set before serving.

These little friand cakes are extremely easy to eat, let me tell you! The colour you achieve when baking with matcha green tea is just wonderful. You don't need much to impart a subtle flavour and I find that the lime really brings it out. Lemon also works really well, but I expect purists would just prefer them with matcha tea alone!

Matcha tea, lime and almond friands

115 g/1 stick butter, melted
75 g/scant ⅔ cup plain/ all-purpose flour
200 g/1⅓ cups icing/ confectioners' sugar, plus extra for dusting
2 teaspoons matcha tea powder
½ teaspoon baking powder
100 g/1 cup ground almonds
a pinch of salt
zest of 1 lime
6 egg whites
16–18 whole raspberries
50 g/⅔ cup nibbed or flaked/slivered almonds

2 x 12-hole friand pans

Makes 16–18

Preheat the oven to 180°C (350°F) Gas 4.

Melt the butter in a small pan over a low heat. Brush the insides of the pans with a little of the melted butter and dust with plain/all-purpose flour to coat. Tap the pans upside down on the work surface to knock out any excess flour.

Return the butter to a gentle heat and continue to cook until it starts to turn a pale nutty brown. Remove from the heat sooner rather than later as it will continue to cook in the residual heat from the pan. Leave to cool slightly. Sift the remaining flour, icing/ confectioners' sugar, matcha tea powder, ground almonds and a pinch of salt into a large mixing bowl. Add the grated lime zest, mix to combine and make a well in the middle of the dry ingredients.

In another bowl, whisk the egg whites until they are foamy and light but will not yet hold anything like a peak. Pour into the dry ingredients along with the melted brown butter and fold in using a large metal spoon or rubber spatula until thoroughly combined. Spoon the batter into the prepared pans, filling each one almost to the top until the mixture is used. Press a raspberry into each cake and scatter with a few nibbed almonds. Bake on the middle shelf of the preheated oven for 10 minutes until well risen and golden brown at the edges.

Turn the friands out of the pans and onto a wire rack. Dust with icing/confectioners' sugar to serve.

Menu Planners

Birthday party

'Coronation' chicken sandwiches
with pickled red onion (page 63)

The Ritz Fruited scones (page 25)

Raspberry and rose party hearts
(page 42)

Jam and coconut cakes (page 108)

Cherry and almond Bakewell tarts
(page 30)

Passionfruit meringue tarts (page 49)

Victoria sponge *with strawberry
jam and vanilla buttercream* (page 34)

Anniversary celebration

Smoked salmon sandwiches
with whipped cream cheese (page 18)

Gougères (page 122)

Black Forest fondant fancies (page 111)

Cherry and almond Bakewell tarts
(page 30)

Mango and coconut millefeuilles (page 79)

Caramelized pineapple 'upside down' cakes
(page 84)

Prosecco, lime and mint jellies (page 68)

Apple crumble and custard tartlets (page 155)

Mother's Day tea

Smoked salmon sandwiches
with whipped cream cheese (page 18)

The Ritz Fruited scones (page 25)

Earl Grey and lemon teapots (page 151)

Passionfruit 'jaffa' cakes (page 71)

Vanilla and chocolate Battenberg (page 107)

Prosecco, lime and mint jellies (page 68)

Buttermilk panna cotta *with strawberry
compote and orange crumble* (page 160)

Strawberries and cream cakes (page 75)

Father's Day tea

Chicken liver parfait *with thyme and onion
confit and fluted brioche* (page 147)

Fig and ricotta crispbreads *with pistachios,
mint and pomegranate molasses* (page 121)

Gougères (page 122)

Blueberry and buttermilk scones
with honeycomb butter (page 41)

PBJ cookie sandwiches (page 99)

Gramercy Tavern's Sour cherry cake
(page 112)

Triple chocolate cookies (page 96)

Dark chocolate and yuzu teacakes (page 159)

Garden party

Cucumber sandwiches
with yuzu and chive butter (page 21)

Pulled ham hock sandwiches
with piccalilli mayonnaise (page 60)

Triple cheese scones
with whipped mustard butter (page 88)

St Clement's posset *with basil sablés*
(page 67)

Belmond Le Manoir aux Quat'Saisons
Apricot and lavender almondine (page 163)

The Dorchester 'Beehive' tarts (page 45)

Fireside feast

Red wine poached pear, Stilton and endive
on walnut bread (page 92)

Devilled egg mayonnaise
sandwiches *with micro herbs* (page 21)

Chocolate and cherry scones *with
Kirsch and vanilla Chantilly cream*
(page 126)

Malty egg custard tarts (page 100)

Spiced pumpkin apple cakes (page 104)

Carrot cake (page 53)

Marmalade Madeira cakes *with
macadamias, hazelnuts and almonds*
(page 83)

Festive canapés

Roast beef sandwiches (page 18)

Bloody Mary shrimp sandwich (page 38)

Gougères (page 122)

Eccles cakes *with Pedro Ximénez
and Manchego cheese* (page 95)

Chocolate and cherry scones *with
Kirsch and vanilla Chantilly cream*
(page 126)

Harrods Mince pie brownies (page 134)

Spiced chocolate domes *with brandy-soaked
raisins and cacao nibs* (page 141)

Prosecco, lime and mint jellies (page 68)

Strawberry and sherry trifles (page 138)

Hazelnut, apricot and vanilla roulade
(page 137)

Treacle tarts *with ginger cake and orange*
(page 133)

Veronica's gingerbreads (page 129)

Champagne tea

Fig and ricotta crispbreads *with pistachios, mint and pomegranate molasses* (page 121)

Eccles cakes *with Pedro Ximénez and Manchego cheese* (page 95)

Coffee and caramel éclairs (page 156)

Lemon and polenta drizzle cakes (page 50)

Prosecco, lime and mint jellies (page 68)

Strawberry and champagne tarts (page 164)

Rhubarb and custard macarons (page 152)

Belmond Le Manoir aux Quat'Saisons Apricot and lavender almondine (page 163)

Breakfast tea

Bloody Mary shrimp sandwich (page 38)

Smoked salmon sandwiches *with whipped cream cheese* (page 18)

Blueberry and buttermilk scones *with honeycomb butter* (page 41)

Earl Grey and lemon teapots (page 151)

Simple vanilla shortbreads (page 29)

Coffee, walnut and cardamon cake (page 115)

Fruit cake *with an orange glaze* (page 57)

Bridal shower

Fig and ricotta crispbreads *with pistachios, mint and pomegranate molasses* (page 121)

Roasted walnut and miso shortbread (page 148)

Gougères (page 122)

The Ritz Fruited scones (page 25)

Chocolate and cherry tarts (page 72)

The Berkeley Pistachio and strawberry délices (page 76)

Matcha tea, lime and almond friands (page 167)

Marmalade Madeira cakes *with macadamias, hazelnuts and almonds* (page 83)

Gentleman's tea

Pastrami and emmental open sandwich *with thousand-island coleslaw* (page 91)

Triple cheese scones *with whipped mustard butter* (page 88)

Olive and anchovy whirls (page 118)

Eccles cakes *with Pedro Ximénez and Manchego cheese* (page 95)

Cherry and almond Bakewell tarts (page 30)

Mocha mini cakes (page 54)

Rum savarin *with charred pineapple and coconut chantilly* (page 80)

Retro tea

Devilled egg mayonnaise
sandwiches *with micro herbs* (page 21)

Classic scones (page 22)

Simple vanilla shortbreads (page 29)

Golden ginger custard creams (page 130)

Jam tarts (page 46)

Cherry and almond Bakewell tarts
(page 30)

Nans' Welsh cakes (page 125)

Fruit cake *with an orange glaze* (page 57)

Strawberry and sherry trifles (page 138)

Thanksgiving treats

Red wine poached pear, Stilton and endive
on walnut bread (page 92)

Triple cheese scones
with whipped mustard butter (page 88)

Veronica's gingerbreads (page 129)

PBJ cookie sandwiches (page 99)

Pumpkin and pecan pies (page 103)

Malty egg custard tarts (page 100)

Vanilla and chocolate Battenberg (page 107)

Baby shower

Cucumber sandwiches
with yuzu and chive butter (page 21)

Devilled egg mayonnaise
sandwiches *with micro herbs* (page 21)

Triple cheese scones
with whipped mustard butter (page 88)

Viennese whirls (page 26)

Chocolate and peanut butter délices
(page 33)

Cherry and almond Bakewell tarts
(page 30)

Rhubarb and custard macarons (page 152)

Resources

UK

INGREDIENTS

Cacao Barry
www.cacao-barry.com
+ 44 (0) 1295 224 700
Cacao Barry specialist, luxury chocolate is available at their website. Also available to buy are decorations, truffle spheres, chocolate-making equipment and packaging.

Callebaut
www.callebaut.com
+ 44 (0) 1295 224 700
Sister company to Cacao Barry (above), producing finest quality Belgian chocolates.

Chocolate Trading Company
www.chocolatetradingco.com
+44 (0) 1625 508 224
Specialists in luxury chocolate selling gourmet gifts, bars, ingredients, baking transfer sheets and decorations online.

Home Chocolate Factory
www.homechocolatefactory.com
+44 (0) 20 8450 1523
Online sellers to the UK of specialist equipment for chocolatiers including a wide range of ingredients such as freeze-dried fruits, couverture, shells and baking transfer sheets, as well as moulds and packaging. Includes recipes ideas and technical advice.

Keylink
www.keylink.org
+44 (0) 1142 455 400
'One-stop shop for everyone working with chocolate'. A wide range of ingredients, decorations, equipment and packaging available for delivery in the UK and Europe.

Kingdom Coffee
www.kingdomcoffee.co.uk
Purveyors of Fairtrade tea, coffee, equipment and sundries.

Modernist Pantry
www.modernistpantry.com
For very hard-to-find ingredients including platinum-grade leaf gelatin.

Ndali Vanilla
www.ndali.net
Ndali Vanilla produces exquisite Fairtrade organic vanilla beans/pods and vanilla powder, and Fairtrade vanilla extract. Availiable in good-quality food stores and online.

Sous Chef
www.souschef.co.uk
+ 44 (0) 20 7998 5066
Online resource for cooks, offering ingredients, equipment, tableware and gifts inspired by leading chefs and international cuisine.

Tate & Lyle Sugars
www.tasteandsmile.com
Quality sugar products available to buy from food halls and supermarkets in the UK and online.

Waitrose
www.waitrose.com
+ 44 (0) 1344 825 232
Supermarket in the UK, selling fresh, quality food and drink. Stores across the UK and stockists of a wide range of baking ingredients and other quality food products.

Whole Foods
www.wholefoodsmarket.com
+44 (0) 20 7368 6100
Shop for high-quality natural and organic foods, committed to sustainable agriculture.

BAKING AND GENERAL KITCHEN EQUIPMENT

Amazon
www.amazon.co.uk
Useful online marketplace for hard-to-find ingredients and equipment.

Baker & Maker
www.bakerandmaker.com
+44 (0) 20 7378 9228
Online shop for baking and craft equipment including decorations, craft-inspired apparel and homewares, and many other items.

Continental Chef Supplies
www.chefs.net
+44 (0) 808 1001 777
Suppliers of catering equipment and clothing including dessert frames, chocolate moulds and other specialist baking equipment.

John Lewis
www.johnlewis.com
+44 (0) 1698 545 454
UK department store stocking everything from clothing to kitchen equipment, appliances and linen.

Lakeland Ltd
www.lakeland.co.uk
+44 (0) 1539 488 100
'The home of creative kitchenware' and stockists of a wide range of baking equipment such as cake pans, spatulas, chocolate moulds and other useful equipment.

Smeg
www.smeguk.com
+39 (0) 522 821 1
Sellers of premium domestic appliances and equipment.

Thermapen
www.thermapen.co.uk
An indispensable tool for measuring precise temperatures when baking and working with chocolate.

CHEF'S CLOTHING AND APRONS

Continental Chef Supplies
www.chefs.net
+44 (0) 808 1001 777
Suppliers of catering equipment and clothing including dessert frames and chocolate moulds.

Oliver Harvey
www.oliverharvey.co.uk
+44 (0) 161 342 1032
British producer of tailored chef's clothing, designed to withstand the rigours of a professional kitchen.

TUTORIALS AND INSPIRATION

Academy of Chocolate
www.academyofchocolate.org.uk
Founded in 2005 by five of Britain's leading chocolate professionals, united in the belief that eating fine chocolate is one of life's great pleasures. Members meet to taste, discuss, demonstrate and debate issues regarding the journey from bean to bar.

The Chocolate Academy™
www.chocolate-academy.com
+44 (0) 1295 224 755
Teaching and training centres around the globe for artisans and professionals who want to improve their skills in chocolate and learn about new trends, techniques and recipes.

MISCELLANEOUS

Etsy
www.etsy.com
An online marketplace where people around the world make, design and sell unique goods, from tableware and clothing to bespoke invitations and decorations.

Not On The High Street
www.notonthehighstreet.com
Host to online sellers from around the world, creating tableware, linen, decoration and invitations.

Pear Paper Company
www.pearpaperco.com
Wedding and events stationery for happy occasions, based in the UK.

US

INGREDIENTS

Cacao Barry & Callebaut
www.cacao-barry.com
www.callebaut.com
+1 (312) 496 7300
As above.

King Arthur Flour
www.kingarthurflour.com
+1 (800) 827 6836
All types of flour and sugar for all your baking needs, plus spices (including vanilla bean paste), baking sheets and pans galore. The experts at their Baker's Hotline will answer your baking questions, too.

L. A. Burdick Chocolate
www.burdickchocolate.com
+1 (888) 229 2419
For cocoa powder, chocolate, almond paste and nut flours as well as European-style chocolates, contact chocolate confiseur L. A. Burdick, based in Walpole, New Hampshire.

Nielsen Massey
www.nielsenmassey.com
+1 (800) 525 7873
Illinois-based manufacturers of pure vanilla extracts and other food flavourings from peppermint to rose water.

North Bay Trading Co.
www.northbaytrading.com
+1 (800) 348 0164
Delivers high-quality ingredients on a personal and commercial scale in the US.

Teas Etc
www.teasetc.com
+1 (800) 832 1126
World-class black, oolong, green, herbal and rooibos teas. Certified organic teas as well.

Whole Foods
www.wholefoodsmarket.com
+1 (844) 936 2273
As above.

BAKING AND GENERAL KITCHEN EQUIPMENT

Amazon
www.amazon.com
As above.

Cooks Dream
www.cooksdream.com
+1 (866) 285 2665
Explore the site for baking pans of all shapes and size, royal icing mix, food coloring, pastry bags and tips and other baking supplies.

Crate & Barrel
www.crateandbarrel.com
+1 (630) 369 4464
US department store stocking everything from clothing to kitchen equipment, appliances and stationery.

La Cuisine: The Cook's Resource™
www.lacuisineus.com
+1 (703) 836 8925
For a wide variety of finest-quality baking ingredients and bakeware, explore the website of this independently owned cooking store located in historic Alexandria, Virginia. The knowledgeable experts at the Baker's Hotline will answer all your questions.

Smeg
www.smeg.com
+39 (0) 522 821 1
As above.

TUTORIALS AND INSPIRATION

The Chocolate Academy™
www.chocolate-academy.com
+ 1 (312) 496 7427
As above.

Index

Acknowledgments

A massive continued thanks to all of you who have enabled me to write this book. The wonderful team at Ryland Peters & Small; Cindy, Julia, Leslie, Steph and Megan. My amazing new photographer Matt Russell and his assistant Ollie Coleman – thank you for the laughs and for capturing my food so beautifully. To my wonderful recipe tester and writer, Annie for simply being amazing and getting my way of thinking. Big thanks to my food stylists; Jack and Kathy for excellent crumbs technique and much more. Big thanks to all my guest chefs and pastry chefs; John Williams MBE (The Ritz London), Mourad Khiat (The Berkeley), Benoit Blin MCA (Belmond Le Manoir aux Quat'Saisons), Miro Uskokovic (Gramercy Tavern), Markus Bohr (Harrods) and David Girard (The Dorchester). Thanks also to Bruce Langlands of Harrods, Hannah Pickett of The Ritz London, Peter Sidwell, Sarah Selzer and Kilner for the fantastic jars, Ian Mitchell from Oliver Harvey for the wonderful aprons, Jonathan Simms from Pernod Ricard for the simply delectable Perriet Jouet champagne and Clare Edwards and the team from Smeg for the fab new stand mixer and finally to Johnny Iuzzini for such a wonderful endorsement!

There are so many more people to thank who have continued to walk the journey with me but most importantly you all know who you are. I am so blessed to call you family and friends – love and thanks to you all. Finally, JC, you continue to be a Superstar and rock my world.